Money Management

Become a Master in a Short Time on How to Create a Budget, Save Your Money and Get Out of Debt while Building Your Financial Freedom

Complete Volume

By

Income Mastery

Money Management

Become a Master in a Short Time on How to Create a Budget, Save Your Money and Get Out of Debt while Building Your Financial Freedom

Volume 1

Money Management

Become a Master in a Short Time on How to Create a Budget, Save Your Money and Get Out of Debt while Building Your Financial Freedom

Volume 2

Money Management

Become a Master in a Short Time on How to Create a Budget, Save Your Money and Get Out of Debt while Building Your Financial Freedom

Volume 3

competence. There are no scenarios in which the publisher or author of this book can be held responsible for any difficulties or damages that may occur to them after making the information presented here.

In addition, the information on the following pages is intended for informational purposes only and should therefore be regarded as universal. As befits its nature, it is presented without warranty with respect to its prolonged validity or provisional quality. The trademarks mentioned are made without written consent and can in no way be considered as sponsorship of the same.

Table of Contents

Money Management: Volume 1

Become a Master in a Short Time on How to Create a Budget, Save Your Money and Get Out of Debt while Building Your Financial Freedom

By

Income Mastery

INTRODUCTION

As you can see, it's all about the administrative fundamentals you have to take into account, such as your production, what you really produce, and what your offer is, or rather... What are you going to bid? After that, who's going to be the demanding public of your offer? I mean, who's going to need your product?

It seems long and tedious, but as you can see, it is a well-structured and defined planning process which will allow you to determine how much you need to invest and how much you can expect to earn in a period of time that you will establish according to the process of your production and the supply side of the market.

Remember that budgets can be public or private, and each budget is conditioned by clear and precise goals in a given time. Let's use a clear example: suppose you want to go on a trip with a family member or friend to a place close to your country or region. In principle, you will already be, in a decisive way, establishing the main objective: to go on a trip to a place in your country or region. This makes it a feasible goal, as you will be within your budget, if you are working and earning an income that will allow you to make that trip. Next, you will need to prioritize the steps to achieve that objective or goal. This involves following carefully some specific rules for achieving your goal which, as part of a plan, makes you commit yourself to fulfill it adequately because, in the end, you expect to achieve a positive result. Therefore, you will also have the participation of that person who will accompany you, and given certain steps you will include what actions the other person must perform to be part of your planned strategy in the time you want to achieve it. Once you have completed the steps and procedures to achieve your objective, you will have to make a decision which will be preponderant to delimit its scope.

Budgets, like most planned processes, are generally flexible and subject to modifications and unforeseen situations. That's why taking the above example, you may have realized that you still need to complete some fees to cover expenses necessary for your trip, or that suddenly you have exceeded your savings expectations and you have something left for buying some souvenirs or products that you want alternately to include in your trip.

With the example of the trip, we have touched on two other important terms: income and expenses or expenditures. To define an income, we can visualize an employee who offers services in a company; the payment he receives for these services is what is called income. This employee can receive income from other sources, such as tips, commissions, percentages or bonuses for production. This additional income will motivate the employee to improve and expand their production in such a way that they will look for tools with which they can achieve that goal. As you will see, this budgetary process is very much linked to our lives, and therefore it depends on our judgment to make the right decisions and stay in the production market; in the previous case, offering a service.

It may sound fortuitous to you that a particular person can earn an additional income, but, in fact, it is not; what happens is that when a person is in situations of self-demanding, he forced himself, in an "unconscious" and sometimes "intentional" way, to make and offer alternatives for overcoming and achieving a greater scope of net profits for his subsistence. Subsistence is understood as those means that are necessary to support oneself, in this case economically speaking. However, it must be clarified that subsistence also depends on planning and not only on improvisation, since it will never be linked as something fortuitous or improvised. Human beings tend to have instantaneous thoughts, which flow just like words in micro-thousandths of a second; in this process we let productive ideas flow into our minds and take them to action in a time we consider relevant. We can take this analogy in the same way for the budget, because when we clearly establish our goals and actions to follow, we define how we are going to achieve it, so as to then check our results with what we have planned; this way we are be able to improve our budget plan, as what we seek is to always have a positive balance and never expect a negative result because it would make us feel disappointed and discouraged, and always having as the final goal what we want to achieve in a determined period of time.

What are the differences between the budget of a private company and a public organization or institution? At first glance, the answer to this question seems easy, but one of the key points of the answer are incomes and expenses or expenditure, as mentioned in a previous example. Public institutions as well as private companies seek to meet goals or objectives but with a clear differentiation: they are subject to a cost plan and therefore, they are linked to a resource much more important than material goods, and it's is about human and qualified personnel. Without this resource, organizations and institutions would be unable to function properly and would not be successful in achieving their objectives.

If a food street vendor did not take into account the occurrence of plaintiffs in a place where he wanted to bid and offer his product, it would obviously be very difficult to achieve his sales targets, and that would lead to an inevitable failure and consequently, to a loss that will be reflected in his income.

The human factor as a resource is important to establish the action limit of the plans proposed for the achievement of the goals.

Another point to take into account is to determine how much responsibility will rely on the members of an organization to achieve the final goals. If you and your team are not clear about what you need to achieve, why you need to achieve it, and how you are going to do so, you will surely be creating an unstable environment for the direction and control of the actions stated from the beginning.

Let us then begin to prepare in a practical way how to elaborate a budget and improve our finances in our daily lives.

Chapter 1: Determine your income and expenses

How much income do you generate per month? It is usually a very difficult question to answer, but if you dare to determine it, you must also define how much net gain you will be able to obtain after that time. Once the answer to the first question is achieved, you can then calculate how much allocate to the expenses that we will be dealing with in the next section. To accurately determine your income, you must write down in an orderly and organized manner the money you earn for your effort and the time required to earn it. Your work is worth, as long as it is delimited in a space of time that will give the definitive characteristic to this work.

Begin with the income of greatest benefit, i.e. those whose value is greater within the indicated study time (a month); then continue with those of lesser value, taking the first one as reference. Once elaborated this classification, it is recommended to make a summation throughout the whole month taken a delimiting period of time for our record of income, to what we will denominate: monthly income record or income record of X month.

It is important to emphasize the accessibility to your income; even if you do not believe it, most of the income, as well as payments, that can be taken place in a store or trade, can be given in different ways: bank deposit, cash in current currency, checks, and the like. These different ways of receiving payment for your work make that, in a way, the income does not seem "real". If you pay attention to this, when you receive a bank deposit, it may be subject to the bank charging commissions, which causes your income smaller little by little. It is not intended or meant to imply that banks are bad for your income; on the contrary, they are usually a good way to plan your financial life and establish better economic projects. The purpose of this information is to determine the reality of the income received, so let's take an example: suppose you receive a job payment in a different currency from the official one; obviously, by changing it to your local currency, you will have a price that, in the end, will determine what payment has actually been received. This is true for people who, when they charge a service in foreign currencies, have an expectation of the cost of their currency, and are therefore conditioned by the movement of the supply and demand of prices of that currency.

Consequently, many people who receive an income in foreign currency risk that the price of that currency will be favorable when changing to their local currency, hoping to receive a higher income. Obviously, this is not a very common case in those countries where there are regulations for the entry of foreign currency.

Now that you can determine what your income is, then we can determine the expenses, which are going to be as important as the income; in fact, without them, we won't know what our real and exact net benefits are.

Expenses are as complex as our emotions and needs, so we must have greater accuracy for the recording and description of such information. Fundamentally, according to the administrative texts commonly used in universities, expenditures or expenses should be established based on a scale of categories of priority and importance. In this way, we have expenses that are a priority, that is to say, that we must obligatorily pay them, or else it will be much more difficult for us to carry out our goals in the determined period of time, and other types of expenses which, although they are not so necessary, usually are included in the set of expenses that derive from the priority ones.

Consider as a priority expense the basic home support services: electricity, water, telephone, gas, food, housing loan, rent/ room rent, apartment or house. While the non-priority, which we could call secondary, can be transportation, clothing, shoes, payment of commissions or external work such as repairs, cell phone plans, tv, internet, meals outside home and others. Of these last types of expenses come a smaller and feared group, since it causes a decrease in the personal income; they are known as "ant expenses", and they must be carefully examined. To avoid them is an obligation for any person who needs to improve and to precise effectively their income register. These expenses represent 15% of our total expense and, when added together, generate losses that affect our ability to save and invest. An example of this is those expenses that are made out of "whim" or caprice in situations or moments in which they are not essential, and they only generate superficial pleasure and satisfaction; this is the case of paying for a taxi when, in reality, you can resort to cheaper services, outing to the cinema just for the satisfaction and pleasure of seeing the latest movie premiere, the payment of commissions for late card payments, basic services and others. And so, there is another series of expenses of the same type that damage our initiative and monetary utility.

Once we have written down our expenses in a decisive way, it is important to make the sum of those expenses by ordering them from greater to lesser. In the description of each expense, we must take into account the period of its recurrence: that is, if it monthly, weekly, and the like. If we have more expenditures than revenues, we should not be discouraged, because that is when we must take action through a strategic plan to eliminate unnecessary expenses and increase the capacity to produce higher revenues.

The above lists can be compiled using summary or spreadsheets such as those of office programs and writing down as much accurate information as possible to make decisions that will help improve the situation we have determined. It is possible that all this information will serve us as a study for our financial development strategy, and will make us think well when it comes to spending the money that we have earned arduously and with much sacrifice.

Another recommendation when writing down expenses is to classify them according to their need, for example household expenses, personal expenses, food, etc.

Chapter 2: Deciding and using a control tool

After writing down your expenses and income, it is time to determine exactly what or which control tool will be necessary to reduce expenses and increase income. Make a simple calculation to know what our net profit is; if the profit is positive, we will have a surplus, if it is negative, there will be a deficit.

If we have a surplus, the strategy to use will depend on our needs. For some people, the best option would be to invest the profit obtained from the subtraction of expenditures; for others, it would be simply to follow a saving plan to acquire a necessary good.

A very common control tool is the shopping list; another it is a production or sales budget, if it is the case to increase revenue.

For others, the control of their budget is carried out by means of templates of updated records of data of expenditure and income. Regardless of the chosen tool, the purpose will always be to control both the expense and income generated in the time required for that purpose.

Once again, when determining whether there is more expenditure than income, the first thing to do is to start reducing those of high incidence that drastically decrease your income. There are expenses that are fixed and you cannot do without them; however, we could look for alternatives that reduce their output, as for example buy cheaper or on sale products, travel in a cheaper means of transport, avoid the excessive use of basic services at home, such as telephone, electricity, water and others. There are other expenses called "ant expenses" whose impact on the budget are very catastrophic and harm the personal and family welfare, this is the case of dining out or buying in restaurants or cafes. The best control tools for recording expenses and revenues are data collection templates combined with written or date-printed expenses backup, incurred in a weekly or monthly period.

To use or apply these templates you need sophisticated applications such as spreadsheets; office software tools are very useful for these cases, given their versatility from a computational approach. Also, a database record could be used, as well as saved receipts, ballots and consumption invoices. In the same way, databases connected with graphical applications could be developed so as to show graphs and summaries of all our expense and income distributed in a time determined by the system. There are other tools as simple as the previous ones, such as financial and accounting management software, which facilitate the registration task without specifying the required fields, as such software take what they need form the information provided by the user, and process it into reports and calculations that are then displayed on screen when needed and required by the operator.

Obviously, for those who do not trust electronic tools completely, they can continue using pencil and notebook, and there insert the necessary backups so as then project the register results to make decisions to improve the results obtained.

Many experts usually recommend visiting the bank to consult and obtain financial advice about your money, but this is worth when you have a base capital to manage your finances. However, there are people who often could give you, on their own initiative, free help to your interest in saving and having better results on your future income by giving advice applicable based on your own interests, such as new ways of earning an income through small investments, or even how to carry out a saving plan to obtain excellent results in the future.

Returning to the subject of software, we find good options both online and offline; keep always in mind the fact that many take into account the total income and expenditure to give a council or reference on your financial management. A very productive couple long ago wanted to know how it was possible that their income faded so quickly, when they could have had a very good and regular income throughout the year; they realized that after obtaining a certain income, they spent approximately 90% of what they had generated and therefore, there was no progress in their savings. This had very negative consequences, and thus much tension in their relationship. After applying registration techniques and detecting where their funds were going, they were able to take more decisive actions and also achieved a saving goal that grew more and more over time.

All these details could be verified through financial assistance and using a personal financial management software. They carefully reviewed each of their expenditures, and through the calculations made, they observed in detail what these excessive expenses were and what alternatives could be applied. Obviously, this is the importance of using technological tools, because when looking for a certain period of time, it is faster to obtain results, which allows you to make decisions that will help solve the problem. Clearly we know what our biggest problem is: our income disappears, but there are much more interesting problems in which researches will give us more light and reflections on how our income, in which we have put so much effort, is evaporating and how we can prevent it from leaking. That is why we must break down our greatest problem into smaller sub-problems that will allow us to define in an essential way the strategies to be followed to achieve our goal of having greater incomes than expenses in a set period.

It is not easy to have the eager to realize those financial mistakes that have been made for so long, and even trying to improve them, not many people manage to cut them down and change their way of thinking and acting regarding money. It is a challenge for all people, when the will and longing for improvement must prevail in order to sustain the triumph from beginning to end.

In this section, it is worth mentioning a tool described by Nóchez Bonilla on Gestiópolis website, where he defines a technique called the "The tree of income and expenditure", which aims to observe, through an appropriate analysis, economic inputs and outputs (income and expenditure) that negatively influence the budget of any person or social group to seek and implement strategies to increase income (inputs) and decrease expenditure or outputs. The most remarkable thing about this technique is the emphasis it makes on the awareness that people who apply this tool must have, and that they must be willing to change spending habits and apply new ways of earning income. Materially, what it seeks is to educate those who apply it even adapting environmental awareness actions and some other ecological trends, as well as it is expected to be applied in a group setting; this is because the more family members or acquaintances support us in the task of saving and budgeting, the easier it will be to have the eager to move forward and meet the final goal we have set. The following is a brief description of how this technique can be applied in real life and how much time we need for its application.

Initially, we establish a quiet working area with a relaxing atmosphere that stimulates creativity and harmony of thoughts. When several people participate in a session, it is recommended that each one places himself according to his comfort and freedom of development; then we look for recyclable materials to develop the activity, such as bottle caps, paper and cardboard reused or recovered from other elements, wood, pencils, pens and any other thing that serves to understand and register the activity.

At the time of drawing or sketching, the parts of the tree are presented in the following manner: roots, which will be the inputs, the stem, the person or persons from whom the income comes, and the branches represented by the outputs. The thickness and size of each section or part determines the importance of the income or expense, the coarser it is, the greater the importance will be. Once drawn the branches and roots of the tree, we proceed to observe carefully with critical mind both the roots and the branches to identify possible inconsistencies in each part, thinking about the design raised. Thereby, each person makes a call to himself to be aware of the arisen situation; and then, each one seeks to commit himself to a viable solution to strengthen those actions that will make him reach a feasible goal without losing time.

Finally, the participant makes a statistic and a graph of what was observed in order to carry out each of the required steps and writing down those considerations necessary to fulfill his project.

In the end, the purpose of using any of the tools mentioned above is simply to be able to control a personal or family budget; even that of a particular small business, due to its microeconomic structure of operation, is a well-set example for the application of budget control. From now on, it is only necessary to test and adapt each tool according to the needs and priorities established for each financial study.

To conclude, the importance of the tool used will always be to make you think about your ability to solve the expenditure-income problem. Since the greatest problem will always be represented by your expenses, it is necessary that you can pay attention and discover by your own those who have harmed you, and diminish them once and for all by establishing actions that will be carried out step by step to achieve the desired economic balance, with a view to developing and fulfilling yourself.

Chapter 3: In case of a deficit, use a strategy of income and expenditure reduction

Previously, we commented on the expenditure and income registration and control. Special emphasis was placed on expense, since it particularly affects income and causes very negative consequences in the environment of any person, institution or company. We will take into account the fact that being negatively affected by expenses, and duly analyzed by our records, we will employ some strategies that will make our income much more stable even with the possibility to invest in possible options for the future.

Once determined and committed to change your economic situation from deficit to surplus, then we will proceed to establish those actions that will make this a reality and in a determined time. Analyze each expense thoroughly, and establish a recurrence pattern of all of them; determine how necessary it is to use the money in each of them, and place them on a list of priorities; then look for alternatives that allow you to reduce or replace each of them with another that requires less money outflow.

You must begin determining which of your fixed expenses can be significantly reduced. If you really need extra money, you may consider working part-time, moving to a lower-rent apartment, getting a roommate, or renting a room of your home. There may be other saving ideas needed to make your goal a reality; there will always be alternatives for all those expenses that seem unavoidable. Suppose you want to save on electricity, you should become aware of where the most electricity is consumed in your home: it can be an electric stove, a microwave oven, a light bulb on for a long time, the use of high drain appliances which leads into an expensive consumption bill, and obviously you will have more to worry about if you don't take action at all. At first, you may find it difficult to get rid of some unnecessary services such as the Internet plan of your cell phone if you already have one included in your landline or cable television; the same can be done with water consumption, as well as those personal expenses that happen while we are fulfilling others, such as buying unnecessary things during market purchases.

If you still have trouble making ends meet, be sure to prioritize things like your mortgage or rent payment and car payments over unsecured debt, such as credit cards. The last thing you want is to lose your home or car. Not paying your credit card bills will damage your credit score, but it will also make your creditors more willing to negotiate an affordable payment plan with you. If you prefer, you can work with a nonprofit credit counseling agency to negotiate a debt repayment plan on your behalf.

The goal is to, eventually, pay off all the debt that is costing you more in interest than you could reasonably expect to earn by investing that money. For a conservative investor, it would be around 4% 6% for a moderate investor and 8% for someone more aggressive. If the interest rate is below that, it can be considered a good interest rate.

Once you know you can cover all of your expenses, be sure to pay yourself before you pay someone else, as you will automatically save some occasional expenses, such as vacations and holidays, as well as emergencies that may eventually arise. Ideally, you'll also want to do a retirement calculation to make sure you're saving enough for retirement, but for now, at least try to put enough into your employer's retirement plan to get the matching funds that are available to you. That's free money you don't want to leave on the table.

Now that your basic expenses and saving needs are covered, you know how much money you have to spend through no fault of your own on whatever you want, such as shopping, eating out and having fun. You and your spouse may have that amount in cash each month, but when the money runs out, it disappears until the next month. Anything you don't spend can be transferred. The key to conjugal happiness is that neither of you can question how the other spends his or her allotment.

After performing this exercise, our caller discovered that he and his wife could live within their means by simply eating less. They can also use their next bond and a small inheritance to pay off their credit card debt in 3 years.

That will free up money they can use for other goals, such as saving for retirement and making some home arrangements.

The idea is to control your financial future. After all, you know how hard you work for your money.

Some people find it hard to motivate themselves to save, but it's often much easier if you set a goal.

Your first step is to have some emergency savings: money available if you have an emergency, such as a boiler collapse, or if you can't work for a while. Try to get a three-month spending on an easy-access or instant account. Don't worry if you can't save this right away, but keep it as a target to aim at. The best way to save money is to pay some money into a saving account each month. Once you have reserved your emergency fund, possible saving goals to consider may include:

- Buy a car without taking out a loan.

- Take a vacation without having to worry about bills when you return.

- Have some extra money to use while on maternity or paternity leave.

As your savings begin to grow, you can:

- Put more money in your pension. It's a great way to make sure you'll be able to live more comfortably later in life.

- Make an investment plan based on your goals and deadlines.

- Keep records of all your deposits and purchases. Record each in your check register, which the bank will provide to you.

- Print or download your monthly bank statement if you don't already receive one in the mail. If you are doing everything online, there is a software that can facilitate this step, and the budget.

- Do your own calculations of deposits and withdrawals to make sure your bank hasn't missed anything or lost your money. Reconcile line by line, making sure your checking register is the same as your statement.

- Find the final number on each monthly statement and work backwards; verify what has been deleted and what has not. Deposits that have not been settled must be subtracted from their balance. If your checks have not cleared, they should be added back to your balance until they are cleared.

Go line by line and keep in mind the rates you are charged. Seeing them up close may ask you to call and ask that some be removed, which banks will often do if it persists. Also, add any pennies of interest you have received.

Again, if you have access to a computer, or even a smartphone, this process can be automated using a software or financial application, saving you time and frustration. The goal is to review your cash flow, look for errors and learn from what you see.

After you've had the opportunity to control your income and expenses for a month or two, you'll be more aware of the areas that need to be adjusted. Maybe your initial monthly income estimates were off, or maybe you didn't take into account expenses like car repairs or veterinary bills. Make adjustments, but always balance inputs and outputs.

Once you solve all the problems in your budget, you must commit yourself to following it. However, there is no budget forever, so periodic reviews are the key to success.

If you get a promotion, for example, you can increase your discretionary spending and your saving goals. On the other hand, a layoff or fewer work hours could mean cutting back on spending until you restore your income.

Savings should be part of the plan. Financial planners recommend that your savings cover six months of income, enough to make up for a job loss or another emergency. You may find it helpful to open a separate saving account and gradually fund it until you reach your goal. Maintaining a separate account will make it more difficult to raid the emergency fund to cover non-essential items.

As mentioned, an emergency fund is crucial for your financial security. Start by saving 20 dollars per week. In a year, it would be 960 dollars, plus any interest for when the refrigerator stops working or when the transmission explodes.

Experts recommend looking at your tax withholding to find hidden cash. If you receive a large refund each year, you may need to change your marital status to receive additional money in your paycheck for an emergency fund, unless, that is, you are putting your tax return funds into that same fund.

Medical crises in particular can reverse a balanced budget. Negotiate large medical expenses, such as an emergency hospitalization, with the hospital. Almost every hospital negotiates rates. Often, if they are contacted immediately rather than waiting until the amount goes into collection, the hospital or the provider's office can set up a payment plan.

If not, a consolidation of medical bills can help, as it allows you to combine all your medical bills into one lower monthly bill through an agency or a bank loan. Not only does this make it easier for you, but the agreement protects your credit score because you can make payments on time. The disadvantage is that it may take you longer to pay off your debt in full.

Creating a budget is the first step, but keeping the budget is where you start to see real growth in yourself and more duration of your money. Complying with a budget can be a difficult task for people who are not accustomed to spending limits or self-discipline in their finances, so it is important to maintain a positive attitude toward the process.

Staying motivated can help alleviate some of the budget pressures. Consider it non-negotiable to set aside a portion of money month after month so you can expect a relaxing vacation at the end of the year. Finally, set realistic and achievable goals. Start slowly and develop a plan that works for you and your lifestyle.

You should always remember the importance of differentiating between what you want and what you need. You may not be able to get the things you want, but if you try, you'll get what you need.

How are wishes separated from needs? And why bother? For many of us, knowing where to draw the line can mean the difference between creating a successful budget and going bankrupt. So what's the difference? Most needs are synonymous with non-discretionary expenses. They include shelter, which requires payment of rent or a mortgage, and food, which results in grocery bills. There are many other items that are basic and non-negotiable, but the non-negotiable category leaves room for choice.

For example, if you need a car to get to work, you can buy a used vehicle or a new one. The price difference is huge, and a less expensive brand is sure to impress your friends and offer an excellent driving experience. The question is, what can you afford? If you make 50,000 a year, the used car could be yours without stretching your finances. But if you take home 4,000, it's better to keep the used one.

The same rule applies to housing: should you rent a one-bedroom apartment or buy a 40,000-square-foot house? Once again, both offer shelter, but at radically different costs.

There is also a difference between the needs and the elements by which you could live without them. Think about taking a vacation in Thailand instead of a week driving to state parks near your home. Both can offer satisfying and relaxing places to pass your center, but the costs are radically different. Also think about impulse buying. Let's say you go to the home repairs store to buy some lawn fertilizer, and then go back home with a lawn mower you hadn't planned to buy. You may need a new mover, but it's a good idea to research models and prices before reducing your money.

Knowing the difference between wants and needs is the key to a successful budget. You can budget for some impulse purchases or product upgrades, but understand what you're doing, show moderation, and always make sure your budget is balanced.

Chapter 4: Record template use and projected and stable future income management

Budgets are living documents. Just as life is constantly changing, so are the demands on your budget. For that reason, it's a good idea to regularly review your budget to adjust for changes in your income and expense.

What should you consider? On the income side, you must make adjustments if you get an increase or receive an unexpected gain as an inheritance. You must adjust if you lose your job or move to a new one. Getting married or divorced requires a massive reworking of your budget, just like having a child. Sometimes the changes are smaller or temporary, for example, a health insurance co-payment may require a temporary adjustment.

You don't need to revise your entire budget when changes occur. The rent is the rent, and it is unlikely that you will change what you spend each month on your car. But other things are more flexible. If your income falls, you could eat less. If it increases, you could save more, pay off the debt faster, or make a discretionary purchase.

There is no strict rule about when to revise your budget. Some financial consultants suggest doing it constantly; others suggest revising every few months. It's probably a good idea to consider reviewing your budget when life-changing events occur, and setting intervals to adjust for smaller things like inflation and changes in fixed costs.

You should consider making automatic savings as part of your budget. What is an automatic saving? It's the money you set aside to fund an emergency account, pay for Christmas gifts later in the year, or create a college fund for your children.

Automatic savings are best handled by retaining paychecks. If you are saving for retirement and your company offers you a plan, sign up and money will be withheld from your paycheck. Many employers also offer medical and child care saving plans, which are generally tax-exempt. You can also automatically deposit your paycheck into a checking account and then transfer part of the payment to a saving account you don't plan to touch.

There are many strategies for automatic saving. Talk to a financial advisor to learn more about your options and the amount of savings you can afford. Once you implement a plan, keep it. Percentages will vary, but if your company will match contributions to your plan, save at least the maximum amount that will match. Other savings will be largely determined by your income and expense. If you need to withhold 20% of your paycheck to cover rent, be sure to do so. Knowing how much money you need and saving for it will ensure you to cover your expenses and prepare for the future.

Financial experts have presented recommended spending percentages to help people budget for the first time. For example, it is suggested that you spend no more than 30% of your gross monthly income on housing, whether you are renting or owning.

Automobiles are the next largest expense for consumers and probably the greatest temptation to overspend. The best idea is to keep spending between 10% and 15% of your monthly income. Anything beyond that stretches you, especially if a financial emergency arises.

Student loans can be another variable in your monthly budget. There are several income-based payment plans that limit your payments to 10-15% of your income. It's a secure number, but it will often extend payments for a few years and end up costing you a small fortune in interest charges. Try to use 20% of your budget, especially if you don't have a car payment or if you split the rent with roommates.

Other suggested percentages for current expenses include utilities (10%), food (10-15%), and savings (10-15%).

You must commit yourself to staying within the budget until you see results or stability. The best way to do this is to create an annual plan that covers your fixed costs, such as car rental and payment, your seasonal costs, such as gifts and vacations, and your discretionary costs, such as eating out and buying clothes. Work all these things into a 12-month projection and follow it to the letter.

If you find flaws in the plan or if your cash flow changes, you can modify it. Otherwise, try to stick to it. Consider using a software or a budget application to help you. If you discipline yourself, you'll be surprised as debts are paid off, savings grow, and your needs are met.

A budget forecasting approach can include bottom-up, top-down, public-origin, zero-based methods, to name a few. The methodologies for each can be divided into qualitative and quantitative. Qualitative is marked by the judgment of the budget owner, while quantitative is based more mathematically. Consequently, both qualitative and quantitative forecasting methodologies have their respective strengths and weaknesses.

Bias can significantly affect the usefulness of budgeting techniques, so it is important to consider the political aspects of a method. Whether a seller's need is to "play with the system" to increase the likelihood of reaching the bond or senior management needs to achieve objectives to appease investors, bias will often stress the budgeting process.

Simple quantitative methods also have their weaknesses. With a recent customer of mine, during his budget, he was using the average monthly percentage growth of the previous year to forecast product sales. While this is a very reasonable approach, I pointed out that percentage growth fell during the year. The use of that full annual average could lead to a systematic aggressive prognosis if the trend continues or even stabilizes.

As a personal opinion, quantitative processes are the best option to combine with qualitative processes, since they help verify the error verification assumptions based on the previous problems. I recommend a quantitative basis, as it is quick and relatively unbiased. It also explores the company's "function-defining" relationships between expense and revenue, as well as growth trends. Such methods are also more useful for a scenario planning, and can be a good basis for benchmarking and ongoing forecasting.

Because everyone's financial situation is different, you may find that not all categories in spreadsheets are applicable to your income or expenses. You may even recognize that some months are different from others, but after some exercise you should find that you are more prepared for those changes and that you are also accounting for unforeseen expenses.

Although a monthly budget cycle is generally the most reasonable time to establish a personal or family budget, there are many sources of income and expenses that do not perfectly follow a month-to-month schedule.

In that case, calculate how that adds up to more than one month and write it in the appropriate row and column. You may also have certain expected or even recurring expenses that occur more or less frequently than monthly. To count those expenses (such as auto insurance) in your monthly budget, simply calculate the total expense for the calendar year and divide it by 12 to find the "monthly" expense. Write that number in the appropriate row and column.

To get started, gather all your relevant financial statements, such as your pay stubs, credit card bills and any other information that helps you make the best and most accurate estimate of your expected income and expense.

To begin your budget, fill out the monthly budget amount column in the "expense worksheet" as best as you can for the next month. If a certain category does not apply to you, you can simply leave it blank or enter a zero (0) in the box.

Over the course of the month, track your income and expense. At the end of the month, complete the "actual monthly amount" column and compare it to your original estimates. You may have overestimated the amount you would spend on clothing, but you underestimated the amount you would spend eating out. Write down the difference.

You do not need to do this exercise every month, but it is extremely useful at first, as it helps you develop the most accurate monthly budget for future references.

When it comes to money for short-term goals, financial experts say people should focus on saving rather than investing. The money needed in less than three years must be protected from market volatility.

"Short-term investment is where people make mistakes," says Oliver Lee, owner of the Strategic Planning Group in Lake Orion, Michigan. "They see the bright light that says 6 percent and they come in." However, those types of returns generally require people to take risks they shouldn't have with the money they'll need soon.

For short-term goals, try one of the following short-term investments:

> High yield savings accounts.

> Short-term bond funds.

> Fixed income funds.

> Structured notes and others.

People should forget investing the money they may need in less than a year. Instead, find a high yield saving account to keep the money safe and yet available as soon as you need to use it. The money in a saving account is insured, and therefore safe from loss. Money market accounts are another short-term investment option. "While the Fed is currently lowering its rates, there are many money market funds that provide a reasonable return on short-term cash," says Lockyer. They may offer a comparable interest to some others and come with fewer restrictions. However, you may only be allowed to make a limited number of withdrawals from your account each month.

Similarly, fixed income funds offer a relatively stable way to obtain a higher return than that offered through saving or money market accounts. Many of these funds include bonds, but they may also include other securities. Fixed income funds do not offer much in terms of returns, but they are designed to minimize risk and limit losses in a declining market so that they can make good short-term investments.

Michael Windle, a certified retirement income professional and owner of C. Curtis Financial in Plymouth, Michigan, says people sometimes make a mistake thinking they need to save thousands of dollars before they can invest in fixed income or other market funds. "Instead of depositing money in a saving account, just put it in [investments]," he says. Doing this can help them improve their overall performance.

To get money from the one you won't need for at least three years, consider placing at least a portion of it in stock markets. Since most bear markets last nine to 16 months, someone who invests with a five-year time horizon can afford the risk of a bear market. Your investments are likely to recover before cash is needed. However, to be safe, people should start transferring money to fixed income funds and bonds as it nears when it will be used for the intended purpose.

Mark Charnet, founder and CEO of the American Prosperity Group, a financial firm based in Pompton Plains, N.J., says workers should be aware of how much time they have to compensate for the losses they generate. They also need to move their money to more a conservative and less risky investments as they approach retirement.

You must take into account that, in order to improve your income or receipts, you must always assume savings as a method of forecasting in the event that a mandatory need arises. In this way, you will be protecting yourself from unforeseen expenses which will always arise in one way or another, by making imbalances in your income and therefore the budget set in your plan.

Conclusion

By clearly defining the concept of budget, its usefulness and its importance, we have also identified various types of budgets that can be applied according to the type of organization. The mentioned tools will be the key to guide a better theoretical-practical application in the administrative processes of any company or in a personal way. In such way, knowing the main concepts associated to the budgets will be very useful to elaborate predictions of your sales, resources, production, finances, time, optimization and any other activity associated with the normal cycle of your life or of your company.

Entrepreneurship begins precisely by evaluating our life, the actions that help us and those that harm us. Certainly, sometimes it is difficult to accept or identify what everyday things are damaging to us preventing our progress in the consolidation of our goals; it is there where effective decision-making will make the difference between moving forward or stopping. Things do not reach our hands in a magical way; it is necessary to start for our inner peace to ensure right and just decisions for ourselves and for others. Generally, when you earn an income, there is a dilemma between what you like and what you really need. In this sense, we must organize the equitable distribution between basic needs and a fund of money (savings) to cover unforeseen emergencies that may or may not arise today or in the future. Similarly, it is very important to keep a monthly amount of money in order to prepare for a future retirement.

Each day represents a new miracle of life and hope especially when it comes to responding to the dynamics of a society in constant growth; that is how challenges represent a reality to which we must adapt with a clear conviction of growing in the spiritual, familiar and, of course, in the financial field, since only in this way will we gain space for both growth and peace. When we are calm, we are productive in our work spaces, more successful when we are cautious in making really effective decisions and safer in our interpersonal relationships.

Expenses should not overwhelm us, as they can be organized to meet needs without falling into excessive debts that compromise year-end profits. In this way, we can balance the public services of our main home (water, electricity, telephone, gas, toilet, internet, residence, among others), we must also include food, health, transport, recreation, although the latter is not a necessity, because we can share a pleasant time with our family group generating an atmosphere of integration, and I did not mean that it must be an ostentatious expense that compromises the entire income, it can even be a meal at home different from the rest of the other days, an outing to the park or simply eating an ice cream; the important thing is to give a smile to our children, what will give us joy and encouragement in difficult times.

In addition, within our organization, we must not forget the routine health check-ups, which will greatly reduce costly treatments that affect us both psychologically and economically, because the dilemma becomes present again by addressing your health or the fundamental expenses of your family group. Now you must keep in mind that if you forget eating, resting, taking vitamins, and going to the doctor for routine check-ups, you will no longer be a point of support for your family, but a concern as you convalesce in bed. While it is true that some diseases appear and we can do little to prevent them, it is also true that a good state of mind and properly take care of ourselves will decrease the chances of a serious illness to be diagnosed in time, as the best gift for our loved ones is not the most expensive phone, but the warmth of a hug every day, a smile on arrival and a word of encouragement in their most difficult times. We are all very valuable to others, do not be just a memory for not taking care of your health in time.

It is necessary to have a balance between income and expense, so as not to overburden our true capacity to pay. When we realize our reality, we will be able to recognize if our decisions have been correct or, unfortunately, we have made unnecessary expenses. Recognizing the wrong decisions is the first step to allow a significant change in our lives, and make provisions that will allow us to cover expected as well unexpected expenses, which may appear at any time, and only with serenity can we succeed in such unforeseen situations. In the same way, saving is a valuable lesson that we must teach to our children from their first years of life and we begin to develop this by example.

There are expenses that can be cushioned in several months to avoid excessive expenses in a single month; in such a case we can rely on the use of credit cards, which allows us to cover expenses and pay progressively in an accessible amount to our monthly budget, which will allow us to generate a positive record in the eyes of the financial institution in which we have our bank accounts, since in case of requiring an extraordinary credit the secret is to maintain a good payment record, which will show that we can acquire new credits. To do this, we must be responsible at the time of cancellation without waiting for notifications, direct discount from our bank accounts and even less be classified as a delinquent customer.

When observing our payment commitments, we can organize them according to the cut-off date, so we will have to cancel some at the beginning of the month as a priority and others at the end of it; thus, demonstrating to the service provider that we have the ability to meet on the expected date the commitments acquired, avoiding concerns about forgotten expenses. For this, we reflect them on a sheet indicating the assets to the left and the liabilities to the right in order of importance.

An adequate standard of living should be a priority, since if we eat well, we can be productive and reduce the risk of disease. In this sense, it is also necessary to balance work, rest and family sharing, since it is useless to cover all economic needs if they do not meet the affective needs that are present in our day to day life. The complaints often reach such a point in which we cannot fall asleep, which affects our quality of life. The key words are serenity, wisdom and firmness. Serenity is the key when facing situations without despair; wisdom in making decisions and firmness in maintaining the changes that allow us to be happier and more productive. Save not only money but also time by performing simple, everyday tasks in the shortest possible time as this will lessen your worries and increase your peace of mind by demonstrating that the effort was rewarded with success.

This practical text has had as mission to make you understand and value the subject of the budget as part of the administrative processes within the planning, as an irreplaceable instrument to predict the course of the company based on assumptions that allow you to open the way to corporate and business success so that then you can improve your financial life and establish economic values for your development and advancement in the business world. In general, it seems that the budget represents mostly the expense that can or must be made to achieve an economic beneficial goal; remember that, before the rigidity of a budgetary plan, it is necessary to take into account the judgment the planner establishes to define the follow-up criterion on the organization goals.

Money Management: Volume 2

Become a Master in a Short Time on How to Create a Budget, Save Your Money and Get Out of Debt while Building your Financial Freedom

By

Income Mastery

Introduction to Financial Freedom

It is extremely important to build a real budget, have a good attitude, get organized, have goals, and stay motivated. Now let us begin with the path to savings, the payment of our debts and financial freedom. In this book we will teach you how to pay your debts, save and build your financial freedom. We know it sounds complicated, but it's simpler than it sounds.

Let's start by thinking about what financial freedom is for you. What do you want to be financially free for? Do you want to be able to travel whenever you want? Do you want to be your own boss? Do you want to stop working regular office hours of nine to five every day? Do you want to be able to save to buy your apartment or house in cash? Think exactly what you want this financial freedom for and always keep it in mind. Use it as your mantra, remember and think about what you want to achieve every day. Visualize it, write it down, write it down in your diary, write it down in your diary, think about it and write it down every day and think about how you're going to make it. It is very important that we believe in ourselves and are determined and convinced that we are going to achieve it. The mentality is really important, we must be positive and we must know that we are going to achieve it, that the path is going to be a little complicated but that we will achieve it. We must always remain motivated and strive to accomplish what we set out to do.

Now that we know what we want to do and why we want to do it, that is, why we want this freedom, we will have a clearer idea of how and how much to save in our budget. The amount that we must keep will vary according to our objective, that is to say, the amount of savings that we must keep will have to be greater or less depending on what is going to be our objective.

Ten finds that we can achieve financial freedom in several ways, not only by saving more money, we can also generate more money. Do you know how? Keep reading that we will explain it with examples, pages and explain different easy and quick ways to get money in different ways, we can get separate jobs not necessarily in a shop or an office, we can also increase our income in another way.

Is it possible to enjoy your money by having money in the bank and paying all your debts? Of course, we can, can we achieve financial freedom and enjoy our money at the same time? The answer is also yes.

Do you know how to save? Have you ever taken a break before making a purchase? Has anyone taught you how to save? Do you know how to spend? These are fundamental questions we must ask ourselves in order to achieve financial freedom. It seems unreal the question of if we know how to spend, but the truth is that many times we spend on things we don't need, that we already have or that we will never use and we only buy them because we think they could be practical and could serve us at some point. Weird, isn't it? What are you spending on? Why do you have so many debts? These are key questions for changing our habits and becoming more aware of how we are handling our money. Knowing how to save and how to use our money and most of all our credit cards is of utmost importance. Do we really know how to use them? Do you know what the card is giving you as a benefit? Better yet, do you really know how much your credit card interest rate is or how much you have to pay for membership annually? Most people don't know this and this is vital in order to increase our income and have a balance.

Now how do we increase our income and get out of debt if we don't really know how much we earn and spend?

Let's start with the first and most important thing for the creation of our budget, this is the path to financial freedom. We need to do a meticulous financial analysis and really see how we are financially. This means, we must see what debts we have, no matter how small they are, no matter if we can postpone them, we must know what they are and put them in our budget. We must be truly honest with ourselves and review every detail. Let's start by actually calculating how much our income is. For this, we must know exactly what income we have, but we must do this realistically. Let's calculate how much our fixed monthly income is, don't forget that this income must be the same every month and must be fixed. We cannot count the money we think we are going to receive; it is always better to think that we are going to receive less instead of increasing this amount, in this way we can save what we have left to save it or for an emergency fund that is really important. Don't forget to deduct your taxes from your monthly and annual income.

Now we must continue to plan and review the following points, if we already know what our real monthly fixed income is, now we must know what we are spending and what type of expenses we are facing.

We must separate our expenses into two groups, let's start with our indispensable fixed expenses. These are the non-negotiable expenses for us, those that we need to live on, for example, the rent of our house or our apartment, the services that we must pay where we live such as the cost of water, electricity, our cell phone and/or landline, cable, food for our house, gas for our car in case we have one, our health insurance that is really important, among others. We must know how much these expenses are monthly because they are the first thing, we must pay; these are the living expenses that if or if we must pay.

On the other hand, we must also analyze expenditure which is not indispensable. Are there non-essential expenditure? What do we mean by this? Yes, for example, if we go out to work or go for a walk the amount of coffee we buy when we go out, the sandwich in the cafeteria, all the restaurants or delivery's we order when we are lazy cooking. Why do we say that these are expenses that are not indispensable? Because we can reduce them. For example, if you are consuming one coffee a day the five days of the week you are working and the coffee costs five dollars a day, a week is twenty-five dollars, a month is one hundred dollars, a year are one thousand two hundred dollars in coffee. Just as you read it, this is just one example of something that would help you reduce your non-essential expenses. For example, if you have Spotify Premium, if you have a Netflix account, you also have to pay a subscription. Let's say that between these two subscriptions you pay twenty dollars a month, in one year there are two hundred and forty dollars that you pay only in Netflix and Spotify. Add to that the thousand two hundred dollars of daily office coffee, you already have one thousand four hundred and forty dollars in expenses that you could avoid. Am I spending so much money when I go out or for my convenience? That's right. That's right. That's right.

Why are we talking about comfort? Because instead of listening to Spotify we can listen to music on other channels such as YouTube or we can even listen to music on Spotify but on the regular plan that has no cost. The same happens with Netflix, we can watch movies and series not only on Netflix, we can also watch them if we have cable in our house or we can search for different websites that have the same series and movies but have no cost. Of course, the difference is that in Netflix you enter and search for the series and to be able to search for it on a website you will take at least twenty minutes. Here we must make a rational analysis and remember that what we want is more important than that time spent looking for the film, that is, our financial freedom is priceless. We must concentrate on why we should save and why we are making these reductions in subscriptions.

Now, with the data of how much is our real income, not what we think we can earn but what we are actually earning monthly and already knowing how much our indispensable and non-essential expenses are, we must make the subtraction of our income minus our expenses. These numbers must be real in order to calculate this number correctly. We recommend that you look up last year's receipts to get an idea of how much you've spent and, more importantly, on what. This is going to cover us in case we have more consumptions and in case our account is the number that we have budgeted or less, we can save that money or we can destine it to the payment of our debts, that is to say, to the payment of capital of our debts to avoid having interests.

When you make a principal payment, rather than a general payment to that total amount, we avoid paying interest. When we have this calculation ready (our income minus our expenses) we can see how much deficit or surplus we have. After this, we only have to make a monthly budget to see how much we can spend on food, eating out, shopping, among others. In case we do not have a surplus, or we even lack a monthly amount to be able to pay all our debts, we must get and review which are the best options to increase our monthly income. We must know exactly what amount we must increase monthly to avoid falling into debt and pay everything in cash not to use the credit card.

The problem with using a credit card is that many times, or most times, we don't keep in mind how much interest we actually have to pay if we can't pay the full amount of our debt the previous month. Sometimes we go out and start paying small things with the credit card, which hurts us because sometimes we forget or do not pay the full amount then we end up paying many times almost double what we actually spent. Keep these little tips in mind so you can start making more conscious decisions.

Chapter I: Financial freedom

Now, how to achieve financial freedom? Let us remember that if we already have a monthly budget, we must respect it. It is often difficult to stay exactly within the numbers, but we must make every effort to do so. You'll see that once you begin to see your debts diminish and realize the amount of money, you're saving by not drinking a soda, coffee and eating a sandwich during work hours, you'll stop making it happy and look for ways to bring your food or even start taking your instant coffee to work. Of course, it won't taste like coffee in a cafeteria, but your savings account will thank you.

We must keep you focused and always keep in mind why and what we are saving for. If we lose sight of this, it is going to make everything more difficult, this usually happens when we have finished paying our debts, instead of saving, as we see a greater surplus in our savings account than we saw before we begin to spend it without realizing it. When we really rethink and return to the state of consciousness in our expenses that we had before, we realize how much we have spent and it is too late to recover it.

It is really important that we take into account that we must live within our means. Many times, we like to impress other people and for this reason we pay more than we should when we ask for the bill and we want to invite people, suddenly our boss or our colleagues, our family, among others. We do not realize that this is hurting us, that we are not living within our means and that we do not have direction of our expenses, we are simply spending for the sake of spending and that is not good. In the end, we must understand that working more does not mean being debt free, just as having more income does not mean that we will be debt free. We must be aware of our income and of our expenses. What is the use of increasing our income by even 100%, that is, doubling our income if in the end we are also spending twice as much because we think we have money?

We need to be really careful and aware that we can save money, and that there are different types of savings accounts and even investment funds that generate more money because they pay more interest. In other words, money calls money, the more money we have and can save, the more money we can make. Curious, isn't it?

Chapter II: How can we increase our income?

In the following chapters we will show you how to increase our income in order to achieve financial freedom by increasing our income.

When doing your budget did you realize that you need more money to be able to pay your debts and to be able to save? Don't worry, there are many ways to earn more money apart from going to an office eight hours a day.

Let's start, the first and most obvious option is to ask for a raise in work. When to ask for a raise? If you have many years in the company, make an effort and do a good job, it could be a good time to ask for a raise. How to ask? We know that talking to your boss or the person in charge is a little complicated and can be uncomfortable. Before going to the office, check what your functions are, what you are doing in the company, your pending, additional tasks you must perform, the hours you work in the day, among others. Having this information updated and really reviewing what it is that you are doing and have done, is very important because you can also feel more comfortable asking for the increase to the company because you know what your value is, really, what your contribution is.

In addition to this, we might be asked about some of our functions that we don't know, don't remember, or we might think that some additional tasks that we perform are our functions and they are not. This will take you about ten minutes. If you're nervous, practice with a friend. We don't recommend that you talk to your colleagues about this, because you can generate envy and jealousy or a colleague could go ahead and talk to your boss and that's not the idea. It would be best to practice it with someone in your family or someone you trust. This will be better because you will feel more secure and the other person may also give you some idea of how to ask for it. You can measure your tone of voice and already go with a "speech" prepared of what it is that you are going to say. Also, between the two people may think of some questions that your boss might ask you and you could practice the answers that is what we recommend.

If your boss accepts the raise, it would be perfect if you don't work more hours and have this extra raise. Remember that once they accept your increase you will have to update your budget. Do not increase your expenses evidently, you must continue with your fixed expenses and continue reducing your additional expenses that are not necessary. We give you some examples, Netflix and Spotify, we know they help us make our lives more fun in the sense that we don't like to wait, we want to hear the song we like at that moment that's probably why we have Spotify Premium. Remember that these expenses, no matter how small they seem to you, add up, not only monthly but also annually. On the other hand, we like Netflix because we don't have to look for different alternatives on the internet to watch that movie or series that isn't on television. Now, let's remember that they both add up, if you pay 20 dollars a month between the two for example, it is one hundred and forty dollars annually and these are only two of the subscriptions we have, how many subscriptions do you have? That amount can be used to pay your debts, pay your mortgage or better yet, add it to your savings account, remember that the more money in that account the more interest you will have.

Continue to live as if you haven't received an increase, continue with your budget, don't modify it, just add that additional payment to your debts, your savings account or your emergency fund. Is it necessary to make this change and not have that payment? Yeah, it's really important to do this. Don't go into debt again! You are asking for this increase in order to be able to save and to be able to acquire your financial freedom. Don't forget it! It's very easy to lose what our goal is, so think every day about what you want to achieve and how you're going to achieve it, be aware of your purchases and your budget.

On the other hand, if we can't ask for a raise because we're very new, the company isn't having a good time or we just can't do it, we can look to evaluate our options. So, now, let's think, do you want to keep working in the same place? In case you like to work in an office but you know you won't be able to get a raise, you can start looking for another job that can pay you what you would need to be able to cover your debts, save, have an emergency fund and acquire an emergency fund.

Then start looking for jobs that fit you and your profile, check where they fit, whether they fit closer to where you're living or farther away. Why is it so important to evaluate this point? Because you need to see how you're going to move into your new job. For example, if you can walk or cycle to your current job and you can't get to the other job in any of these ways, you will have to subtract this daily cost for the days worked in order to take into account how much our real salary will be. In addition, we must add the stress that it will take us to arrive at our new workplace, we must assess whether this change of job is really worthwhile.

We have to look for a company that is close by, that is not going to overload us with work, that is to say, that we can still have a good schedule or maintain one like the one we had before and that we are not going to be stressed. It is important to take into account our quality of life, what good is it to earn more money in a new company if we go to this really crashed and this will make us sick? If we get sick, remember that we will also have to pay for this treatment. Let's evaluate these points, be honest and realistic. For example, if we could get to the company by bicycle but this would take us forty minutes, even though we get excited and say we're really going to do it, it's going to be our daily sport and this is the way to get there, we have to be honest with ourselves because otherwise we're going to end up taking taxis every day or driving, what will increase our cost in gasoline, mileage what subtracts value to the car, will increase the time in which we must do maintenance to the car because we are going to accumulate mileage faster, will increase our budget for repairs of the car, among others. This is like Monday's excuse start diet or just a potato chip and we end up eating the whole tray, so we have to keep it in mind and be really honest with ourselves. If we're going to do it every day because we're used to getting up earlier and doing sports in the perfect morning, the budget is going to be real, we can get there this way and it won't increase our expenses, but if we know there's a possibility that we can't get up earlier and that we want to drive or go by taxi, then let's not make the change.

You have decided that you do not want to change company, that you want to follow exactly where you are and that you want to get a job somewhere else, you can increase your income by looking for a part-time job, that is, you do not work a full day, full hours, but you work by the hour. There are part-time jobs where you work four hours a day, suddenly you may find one where you can work two more hours. You also have to evaluate what you do during the day, what the tasks are, if you're going to be very tired, if you'll be able to do it and the type of work you're applying for. As we have already told you, it is useless to work eight hours a day, to go to a part-time job four hours more to be able to pay our debts faster if we end up sick, if we end up stressed and most likely sick, or resign because we cannot or worse yet, that we look bad with one or both jobs because we are thinking of the other or we are very tired and stop performing in both.

That's why we really have to meditate and think about which is the best option for us. Do you want to work two hours a day and find a part-time job? Do you know that it won't affect you? Are you sure about that? Then take it and add the additional income to your budget. We will emphasize that this extra money will serve to achieve your financial freedom, not to buy you that pair of new shoes you liked or a new shirt. Put it in your emergency fund because you never know when we might have some kind of mishap.

Chapter III: Work using the digital world and market from home or anywhere in the world

Now, you've decided you don't want to spend any more time in an office, you haven't found any job you want to change to or work part-time in. Do you think you can't generate additional income unless you work in an office? That's false, welcome to the digital age. Work from home, using your computer to generate additional income.

Work from home? All jobs aren't face-to-face? No, you can generate income using only your computer and your skills. Then let's start by giving you some options on how you could generate income from your home.

Are you bilingual, trilingual? How many languages do you speak? Use languages as your added value, as a skill, take it this way and find jobs in the digital marketplace. Where? In the digital world. What do we mean by that? That on the Internet there are a variety of websites and different options and modalities to find work. For example, let's say you speak French, Spanish and English to perfection, that is, you have a good level in these languages and native in one. So, what do I do with these languages? You ask yourself. Easy, we can get text translation jobs on different web pages like Text master, Translated, One-hour translation, among others. This will allow us to work as translators using the languages, we already know; we don't have to learn anything new.

These web pages allow us to work safely, from our computer and during the hours we have time, that is, if we have a week especially loaded with work in our office, that week we can decide not to do this type of work. Just like that? Yes, just like that! Register on different pages so that you are more likely to find more jobs or always have an additional job. Now, if we're going to have this additional work, don't change your budget because you don't know how much you're going to earn on a fixed basis, then, you better write down how much this income is and use it to pay off the principal on your debts, for your emergency fund or to put it in your savings account so that it generates more interest for you.

Apart from these pages, which are usually used strictly for translation work, we recommend that you also enter pages where you are looking for freelancers to work with. What is working as a freelancer? This means that you work for a company, for a person or for a project in a non-attendance way, i.e. remotely. There are companies looking for translators on this type of freelance pages. The good thing about these pages is that they regulate the entire payment process and can defend you in case there is a problem with the client or vice versa. They are very good option to find this type of work.

Now, if you speak different languages you can work as a translator, or you could start teaching one of the languages you speak. You can be a teacher online, there are many websites that are dedicated to hiring teachers to teach remotely as for example to teach English to classes. Not only can you find these websites that allow you to teach English remotely to children's classes, but you can also find other websites that are a space where people come in looking for teachers of different languages. You only have to put the languages you want to teach, a picture of yourself, a description and usually a video. You must also set the price you will charge per hour. It is really important that we take into account the market and the price of other teachers on the pages, we do not want to be very expensive because probably our potential customers will decide to hire someone cheaper than us. We must take this especially into account when we start because we need to be hired, we leave reviews, to show how many classes and how many customers we have had. People think that the more customers we have, the better we must be, this means, that they think there is a correlation between the amount of customers and the quality of our work. We should not have a very low price because people are not going to think we are very good or they will think that we are just starting.

Remember that the perception of our potential customers is really important. For this reason, we must have a competitive price, see the type of videos that other teachers have posted and sell us, we must always take into account our personal marketing when we make our description. Remember that we can also offer a free trial class so that our potential customers know us, this can serve us to hook them, to test our service.

Chapter IV: Working as a freelancer for companies or individuals

Do you not like working as a teacher? Do you feel you have no patience? Are you very shy or do you not speak any additional language? No problem, there are many more options to work freelancer and earn money apart in your extra time, from your home, from your computer and most importantly you can be your own boss. This extra money remember it will take you to financial freedom. Do you like to take pictures or are you a photographer? Sell them!

Now, we have more options. Do you like taking pictures? Start selling them on different websites. Can you sell photos on the internet? Of course, you can sell them on different websites. For example, pages like Shutterstock pay you between twenty and thirty percent per photo downloaded, this means that the better and more photos we have and send, the more chances to increase our income as more people could download our photos more times. Another page that also pays you per download is iStock Photo, they pay approximately fifteen percent for each download. Exclusive collaborators have a higher percentage, they receive between twenty-two percent and forty-five percent. Another option we offer you is Big Stock; they pay thirty percent per individual download. In addition, they will pay you thirty-eight-dollar cents royalty for the sales of customers who have paid a subscription.

These are just three of all the pages you can find that pay you for your photos. Take advantage of them! Search for photos from your previous trips, start looking for how to take good photos, you can take a quick and easy course online. All of this will help you generate more income. Always remember to take into account and see what images are popular on these pages or what type of images are missing so that you do not have so much competition. For example, if there are many photos of couples having dinner drinking wine but there are not enough photos of boyfriends, you might find a niche. Remember that you can take different photos and upload them to these pages and you will not be charged for uploading them or have to pay any maintenance to be on this page. On the contrary, the more photos you can upload to these pages the more possibilities to sell and the more people who could buy your photos.

You don't like selling photos? No problem. Evaluate your skills and start earning money with them. For example, if you like and are good at marketing in your company, use this skill and sell it online. Excuse me? For example, if you work in digital marketing in your company or have experience in this, sell it online and find projects that match your skills. If you have worked in accounting, look for clients in freelancer pages to earn extra money. It's simple. Now, if you think you don't have skills or you're not sure what they are, no problem.

On pages like Coursera you can find free courses where you can learn different skills. You don't get a degree but it comes out that you have completed the course, if you want a degree, you can pay for it and it's not expensive.

It is important that when you find a freelancer job you give a good service so that you can get recommendations. On the other hand, it is also important that you work with people who give you security. For example, check that the websites where you get work have payment policies, usually the work of the freelancer through these pages have the page as an intermediary in case they have a problem. All communication between you and the client must be through the website, the client pays to the website and once you give the advance and the client gives him the ok or give all the work and the client gives him the ok, the website pays you. This avoids fraud, not being paid, being paid late, or being paid a price that was not the one they had agreed upon.

On the other hand, it is also very important that you put a price that is within the market. Before putting our price, we must review how much people who perform a service similar to ours charge to not charge so expensive that we do not want to hire, but so cheap that they think we give a bad service or that we are not professionals.

Chapter V: Selling products on the Internet as your own brand or selling what you no longer use

Do you have a brand of clothes, accessories, hats or something else or do you simply have too many clothes in your room or things that you no longer use? Sell them and earn money! Ah? Can I sell clothes or things of mine online? Of course, you can, all you have to do is make it clear that it's second-hand, that's all and people are going to buy it. How do I do this? There are different websites where you can upload all the products you want to sell, they give you a template, you upload the photos, describe them, put the price and that's it. Now, it is very important that you analyze the competition, that is to say, that you see what the rest of the people or companies are selling on the Internet and that in this way you can have a price that is within the market. For example, let's say you have a pair of shoes that you put on once and that you no longer want to wear. You can sell them through different channels.

Let's start with pages like Amazon or eBay, here you only register as a user, you put your shoes, your policies in case they want to return them, the size of the shoes, the material, among others and you put them on sale. In this way, you would only pay the commission that the page asks you and you would not have to invest any of your money. You can also use the Facebook Marketplace, which is like a large virtual store where people can come

ell things. Apart from that you can also search
rent buying and selling groups in your city and
m there. That way, you can make quick, easy
selling items you don't use.

if you want to sell products and become a company
ave them on websites you can do so. Let's say you
them and you can get hats in your city, pages like
nazon, eBay and Alibaba allow the sale of products as
company and only ask for a sales commission. In other
words, you wouldn't need to spend so much money to
advertise and look for potential customers because these
pages already have traffic of people who trust them and
who want to buy products, they aren't necessarily looking
for hats but if they are looking for other types of
products. What you would have to do is log in and
register as a company, upload your products to the
templates offered by the pages, add the descriptions and
then you would have to wait to see your metrics. What
do we mean by that? That you should see how many
people see your photos and if you're selling any. If not,
what you can do in this case is advertise your product.

It is important that if you want to generate income with
a separate online store create a Facebook page and
Instagram for your company, we also recommend using
Pinterest. You can connect the pages and you can share
your products, articles or you can update and get more
people to follow you. So that you don't spend so much
money, we recommend you ask all your friends to put I
like it, that is, to follow your page in both social

up and sell things. Apart from that you can also search for different buying and selling groups in your city and put them there. That way, you can make quick, easy money selling items you don't use.

Also, if you want to sell products and become a company or have them on websites you can do so. Let's say you like them and you can get hats in your city, pages like Amazon, eBay and Alibaba allow the sale of products as a company and only ask for a sales commission. In other words, you wouldn't need to spend so much money to advertise and look for potential customers because these pages already have traffic of people who trust them and who want to buy products, they aren't necessarily looking for hats but if they are looking for other types of products. What you would have to do is log in and register as a company, upload your products to the templates offered by the pages, add the descriptions and then you would have to wait to see your metrics. What do we mean by that? That you should see how many people see your photos and if you're selling any. If not, what you can do in this case is advertise your product.

It is important that if you want to generate income with a separate online store create a Facebook page and Instagram for your company, we also recommend using Pinterest. You can connect the pages and you can share your products, articles or you can update and get more people to follow you. So that you don't spend so much money, we recommend you ask all your friends to put I like it, that is, to follow your page in both social networks. After this, they could also invite their friends or they can share your page on their walls so that people start following you.

It is important that the content you share is of good quality and is a topic that people may be interested in or that it is a good photo. For example, there are different websites where you can get good quality photos for free like Apixaban and Unsplashed. This makes you have professional photos but you don't pay for them. You should remember that many images, such as those in Google's search engine, are copyrighted and cannot be shared without permission from the person who took them. This is really important because you might have to pay a fine apart from downloading the photo from your social networks for infringing copyright law.

we need to achieve success in our sales. Now, if you have found that people are willing to pay for the course, what you should do is start describing the course. We recommend you start planning it before it becomes more structured, there are things you should think about before you start creating it. Think about how you will deliver the course, you can think if this will be like videos, text and/or audio. This will guide you on what kind of platforms you should start using or could use for your video course. You must also take into account what your audience is.

The target audience is either beginner or advanced. It is necessary to think if later we should make additional courses, if we could have sequels or similar courses. Now that we have this information, we must choose the ideal platform for your virtual course. For example, UDEMY is a very good platform where they sell different courses. Udemy is the platform we recommend because it is a really popular market and can help us start selling our courses. It is much easier to sell them on a popular platform that people already know and trust. Because it is a popular platform, they have different filters for the courses, people who want to buy the courses feel confident because they know that the payments are secure, that they are not going to clone their credit cards and that in case they have a problem with the course they can contact a Udemy support person to help them. This generates much more confidence in the potential customers to whom you want to sell your product.

If you had a website with courses but people don't know you, you don't have many reviews, you don't have many followers, people won't trust you as much. Generate online reputation as a page of courses is complicated, so we recommend that the easiest way to generate money quickly is to find a skill that we have, create a course on a simple platform on which we can sell our product, display it so that people want to buy it. It should be a known page, that people trust you and that has a lot of people traffic. This will facilitate the sale of our course.

Once we have chosen what we are going to teach, we have carried out market research, created the course on the appropriate platform and put it on sale on pages like Udemy, we can easily create money. Remember that always the platforms you must search for to publish must be known, they must already have traffic, they must have payment method for the client and they must have a trajectory. They must be known platforms for you to have more opportunities to sell your course.

Chapter VII: How to Make Money with Virtual Coins Like Bitcoin

Bitcoin is a digital currency that is becoming very well known, this currency can be used to pay for different products on the Internet, you can buy and sell as if they were shares. Have you heard about it? Do you know what it is? This type of virtual currency, Bitcoin, is well known worldwide. We have one more proposal to be able to achieve financial freedom, it is very easy and simple, it is free and it is not laborious to get this money. Next, we will explain you different activities that we can begin to realize to begin to earn money from our computer in a simple way from our house or from any part of the world. This way of making money is fast and direct, and we know how much money we are going to receive according to the type of activity carried out.

First, do you know what bitcoin is? It is a virtual currency that we can use to buy in different stores that are already accepting it as a means of payment. Is it money, does it have value? Yes, and this value is changing. How do I get this money? You may be wondering. Here are some recommendations for you to get this money. Not only can you buy it, but you can get it for free with little effort. Seriously, it's not a lie, I don't have to pay for it. No, there are ways in which you can get it for free on the internet in exchange for performing relatively simple tasks. For example, you can easily start accumulating this currency in trading operations, you can do micro tasks, you can get free coins including bitcoin taps, collect tips, you can invest in bitcoins, sell products and services in bitcoin way and more.

What do we mean by bitcoin trading? We understand that these terms are new and may seem complicated but they are not. Now, about trading, the basic speculation strategy is the one that applies, you must buy the currency when it is with the lowest price you think it could get and then you expect the price to increase to be able to sell it and this will generate a profit. How do I know what is or what will be the price of bitcoin? To know it is of utmost importance to follow the news daily to be able to negotiate with more information at hand and to be able to make wise decisions. We will not be able to know in advance how much the price is or will be, we must stay calm and check the price day by day.

Think about bitcoin as stocks, the price is going to change every day so you will have to revise them daily. Although we believe we know what will happen to this price, we must handle it day after day so we recommend reviewing this information every morning to make informed and accurate decisions. You could also make this negotiation through arbitration, buy cheap in one change and sell at a higher price in another. It is very important that before you buy or start using bitcoin you learn how it works. There are many tutorials on YouTube and a lot of information on the internet that we recommend you research before buying bitcoins.

Now, how do you earn bitcoins without having to buy them? It performs micro tasks. How do I perform micro tasks in order to earn bitcoins? Do micro tasks demand a lot of time? No, they are very simple operations and / or chores that the consumer does and that to the company that is doing it can be worth the difference between selling a product and not selling it. There are some applications where you are paid in bitcoin such as Bituro. This smartphone application pays you in bitcoins after you've done small activities like watching videos, completing surveys, testing applications, and more. These tasks don't take long, they are quite simple and help you earn virtual money. Is this true? Yes, you can go to the different pages that have this opportunity and which many of us are enjoying. These tasks can be done from your cell phone, at any time of the day, during your lunch hour at work or at night. It is very important that you want to do them, you learn to do them and you can do it yourself.

On the other hand, bitcoin reward also allows you to earn money by doing the same type of micro tasking, such as watching videos, completing surveys and other less complicated tasks inclusive. I go in to watch videos, play online games and I can make money? Yeah, and you make money. Another alternative is the hit buckszn. Coin bucks is another application you can use for Smartphone that also allows you to earn bitcoins by performing simple tasks such as playing video games, downloading other types of applications and completing online promotions. This helps companies with their market research, allows them to learn to offer different promotions to people or in this case to segment them.

How do I generate bitcoins through Bitcoin faucets? If you like to play video games, you like to watch videos and you don't mind the ads, these types of tap sites generate their ad revenue and pay a small amount of advertising revenue to their users. All you need to do is register with your bitcoin address and start earning a few bitcoin cents every day. We understand that it is a slow way to earn money but you must remember that it is free, it is simple and it adds up. Another option is also your own bitcoin tap, this will make you earn even more money. The problem is that you will have to search for good traffic on Google or other search engines, you can do this with a good website, or with Google Ads.

We can invest a little money to increase our traffic and have even more income. We must remember that both alternatives are viable, we can start with one, for example, start earning little money and then create our own website to be able to have a little more experience and understand how these websites and bitcoin work.

Still not convinced by Bitcoin? Why don't you believe in this coin yet? Do you think it won't work for you? Aren't you very sure about the value of single coins? We recommend that you go to the library or your computer and see the difference between growing up in a more technological generation or less, relying on the internet and buying things online really changes. Watch videos on

YouTube, read a bit more about the bitcoin coin, there are many pages where they explain how it works with examples and what to do to be able to succeed and win this digital coin or buy it cheaper and be able to sell it more expensive so your profits are higher. I recommend that you start by exploring and earning money on the pages where you are given Bitcoin, so that you begin to understand how Bitcoin works, where you can use this currency and how these pages work, so that later you can make a decision about which type of page is best for you.

Now that you've read all our alternatives to generate more revenue and manage your money well, it's time to increase your profits. There are different ways to increase your income. First you have to see how much you need to save or how much you need to increase your income in order to pay off your debts and achieve your financial freedom. The first option if you like your job and you like going to the office is to ask for a raise. If you're a couple of years old and you do a good job, ask for a raise. This is the easiest option for you to avoid working harder and having to have an additional worry. If your boss says yes, you shouldn't have any trouble adjusting to the previous budget but more money will help you pay off your debts or save in a savings account that gives you interest based on the amount of money in that account.

On the other hand, if you can't ask for a raise because you're very new at work, you can look for another job that pays you more taking into account your mental health as well, that is, take into account the work environment and how far away it is, if you have to travel a lot and if this is going to add stress to your day, hours of transportation and if you have to spend extra to get to work. You can also evaluate what your skills are to be able to look for an additional part-time job, you could work a couple of hours a day in another place but you must take into account that you must also rest and that if you hurry and work too many hours a day you will probably get stressed and end up getting sick for this reason. Now, if you don't want to look for a job or work somewhere else like another office, start looking for a job as a freelancer. Evaluate your skills, see what you're good at and start applying to jobs like this. For example, if you work in digital marketing, apply to community manager or digital marketing jobs in different companies and work remotely.

Many websites have a digital job market and sporadically look for people to complete jobs. Log in, sign up and start looking for a job. You will have to complete your profile and put a price for your work. We recommend that you do this on websites that are known to you and that you read reviews of these pages first. Now, if you don't like working as a freelancer or think you don't have any specific skills, you can take courses on the internet with websites like Coursera, they offer free courses and this will allow you to develop different skills and you can work online. Alternatively, if you speak different languages, look for work remotely, i.e. online, as a translator or teacher of these languages. There are different pages where you can work remotely for institutions, for example, that teach English, you choose your schedule and you get paid monthly.

Now, you can also sign up for different websites that are for private teachers who teach languages via video. Research these options and see if any of them are for you. Didn't like any of the options? Start selling your photos online! Many websites buy photos so they can sell them on their site and this allows you to get a commission every time someone downloads your photos, even can give you royalties. Not thinking about selling your photos? Create an online course and sell it on websites like Udemy. Just look for a platform, create it and you're done. These are just some of the options you will find in the digital market that allows you to work from home, from your computer and generate extra income. This will allow you to get financial freedom and more income quickly and easily. All of these suggested changes will not only change our routine, they will also change our mentality and our relationship and understanding of our finances and our money. It will help us save and this will be simpler than we have always believed, we will be able to reach our goals and achieve financial freedom, we will learn and regain control of our money and time. These small changes in our daily routine will help us reach our financial goals, pay our debts and have our emergency fund.

We shouldn't be stressed about money; we should have better handling. We don't necessarily need that increase or additional work, we must learn to reduce and minimize the additional luxury expenses we have and we must learn to make rational, conscious, planned and unemotional decisions. Start today and change your life! Save today!

Chapter VIII: How to achieve financial freedom at age 40?

We all want to reach this goal, be it at 40, at 50, and why not, at 35... that's why we will now focus on mentioning 5 key points for you to work on your goal of achieving financial freedom at the earliest possible age.

1. Be free to decide

Decide how you want to live your life when you grow up. You'd like to work office hours, or you don't want that for yourself. Likewise, you don't want to depend on someone who constantly tells you what to do. Changing the way, you live is your decision and it's the most important thing.

2. Don't misinterpret the term wealth

The concept of wealth is associated with a very high level of income and with owning property. It's a mistake to associate financial freedom with this idea in your mind. It incorporates a new vision in which time, not money, is the determining factor to increase your economic freedom.

3. Focus on what's important

Focusing on how much you spend rather than how much you earn is what's important. It is no longer a matter of dedicating your life to work but of reducing your efforts to correctly manage your income. Manage your emotions and see what you spend on. Watch your cash flow.

If you save 30% of your salary by limiting your expenses such as not buying a luxurious car, not eating out all the time or constantly and not having ant expenses, which are very dangerous in the long term, among others, you will achieve it.

4. Work for and with pleasure

If you save you will be able to work in what you like, in what makes you happy, since you will not do it for hours nor for money but you will work for satisfaction, and as many hours as you wish in the week. In other words, it is not a question of stopping working completely, but rather, by saving enough capital, you will only need a part of what you earned before and dedicate the rest of your day to what you imagined.

5. Looking for an active income

Having active income, or money from sources that don't require regular work, is an excellent idea and a great challenge. You can write practical books, interesting blogs, generate real estate rentals, etc.

It's important to keep in mind that any one month of that income could go away, although it's also unlikely to go to zero overnight. It's not about accumulating interest over time but getting enough to save day after day.

Chapter IX: It's a matter of attitude

Creating budgets, saving money and getting out of debt is also a matter of attitude. Why do we say this? Because we must want to do it in order to do it! No matter how much we want not to have debts or get out of them, but we mentalize ourselves, make the plan, follow it and change it, it is going to be impossible for us to achieve financial freedom. Remember that all change must come from you. We can guide you and explain how to create budgets, we can recommend which expenses to cut but in the end, it will depend on you to think and achieve freedom. You will see the quantity of benefits and the quality of life that this financial freedom will give you. Remember that the road is not going to be easy, having budgets is difficult and getting jobs on the internet too. If you don't get the first job you're looking for, don't get discouraged, it's always like that, we just have to keep looking and keep applying to different jobs online. Don't get discouraged because nothing's easy.

On the other hand, you're going to need to be motivated to be able to do the extra work and you're going to need to get better organized. We recommend that you use a diary or plan your day, this way, you will be more productive, you will be able to organize yourself in a better way, you will not have so much stress by the additional workload and you will not lose your goal that is the financial freedom. Always keep in mind what you want to achieve, why you are doing this extra work and the fruits it will bring to your life.

If we want to be successful in life, we must learn how to overcome difficult situations and we must always be positive and optimistic. Follow our advice and get rid of your debts, get financial freedom, save more money, even if you want to invest more money to earn more. Take risks but always keep in mind what your goal is. Never forget that reaching our goals is not in straight lines, we will always have to try new things, get out of our comfort zone, we will fail sometimes but more importantly, we will succeed. Begin with this journey to financial freedom, read this book as many times as necessary, take it with you as well as your goals and your reasons. With determination you can achieve what you want, aim for financial freedom, follow your budget, get extra money in any of the ways already explained, and get ready to live in absolute freedom.

Bibliography

Andres N, A. N. (2019, 14 February). Work as a translator - MeVoyalMundo. Recovered October 13, 2019, from https://mevoyalmundo.com/trabajar-como-traductor/

Diego Ortiz, D. O. (2019, October 8). 20 online jobs you can start today without money. Recovered October 13, 2019, from https://www.emprendiendohistorias.com/trabajos-online-ganar-dinero/

20 Internet Jobs ? that you can start TODAY! (2019, 29 June). Recovered October 13, 2019, from https://carlicas.com/trabajos-por-internet/

Money Management: Volume 3

Become a Master in a Short Time on How to Create a Budget, Save Your Money and Get Out of Debt while Building your Financial Freedom

By

Income Mastery

Introduction

Money appeared in the Middle Ages, derived from the word "denarius", which was a silver coin equivalent to 10 aces previously used in the city of Rome, Italy. It is not clear in its historical origin whether money was created spontaneously in the transition from barter to monetary exchange or was invented under the pressure of market forces to facilitate commercial transactions. Although the historical origin of money is not very clear, there is no doubt that we reproduce, extend and consecrate its use day by day. Since the wheel of money began to spin, the controversy surrounding it, its moral considerations, its impact on people, its influence on interpersonal relations, or its integrating effects on the economy, has not ceased.

Today's world is increasingly demanding with regard to the agents that interact between our economy and the rest, in addition to the development of communication and technology, finance are not alien to it leading us to a sea of knowledge that requires us a greater preparation and development of skills to achieve success in the proper management of our resources.

Success in money management can derive from several sources; however, its structure is the key to making meaningful and coherent decisions in daily interactions, with the so-called budget being a fundamental factor. For this reason, this financial tool will be taken into account to reach two important objectives: the result of a logical and efficient series of daily activities to make important personal decisions, in which the word personal means familiar.

The starting point for designing a strategy for investment or spending and finding a way to have additional well-being when managing personal finances. In addition, in this book, we will find how the management of personal finances is not far from the financial organization, concluding that planning is the best motivation and generator of added value in our daily lives.

An effective way to manage money well is through savings, which is a percentage of income that is not spent and is set aside for future needs through various financial mechanisms. In compensation to the saver, the chosen institution pays interest to the account holder on a periodic basis for placing his or her money in the account. When you are told about saving, you immediately think about the debts you have, and it seems absurd to pretend to do so if you can use those funds to pay off those debts. But, anyway, we say to ourselves: "if at the end of the month, after rigorously paying all the bills, the expenses of the month for the house, and if there is no emergency, only then, if there is something left over, I will destine it to saving". This way of thinking leads many to mismanagement of money.

In order to save, the ratio of debt to income should not be breached. You have to keep certain relationships studied. Depending on the income, habits and standard of living of each family group, it can be established with good common sense. The key to the success of this system is that once the money is distributed and an amount is allocated for household living expenses, all expenses, from soap to dog food, will have to come from the amount left over, because there won't be any more money until the next month.

Through the personal financial planning, we will find the aspects that must be taken into account to make a budget, in order to have a frame of reference to make sound financial decisions that allow you to achieve your goals and dreams, in the context of an adequate quality of personal life. By means of financial planning we will be able to achieve attainable goals in a financial, economic and social environment, at the same time of understanding diverse variables that affect the making of financial decisions as the inflation, the taxes and the economic cycles that can affect us externally the planned financial success, additionally, it allows us to visualize and to control the cycle of the finances in our lives, experiencing that to achieve the financial success is the result of our decisions and these are more solid when they are constructed with the aid of the financial planning and all that it implies in the marginal analyses and of opportunity cost in the choices that we make daily.

We will seek to give a small scope on the problems or difficulties that brings the lack of good money management, also will show some strategies, theories and recommendations on how to have a better management and planning of money.

Chapter 1: Administration and money

What is money?

Money is any asset widely used and accepted in transactions involving the transfer of goods and services from one person to another. Economists differentiate between three types of money: commodity money, trust money, and bank money. According to Trust, money is a means at our disposal to improve the quality of our life, ensure the individual greater protection against basic insecurity and in turn give him greater freedom.

- First, commodity money is a good whose value serves as the value of money. Gold coins are an example of consumer money. In most countries, commodity money has been replaced by trust money.

- Second, trust money is an asset, the value of which is less than the value it represents as money. One-dollar bills are an example of trust money because their value as pieces of printed paper is less than their value as money.

- Third, bank money consists of the accounting credit that banks extend to their depositors. Transactions made with checks withdrawn from bank deposits involve the use of bank money.

The functions of money

Money has three main functions:

- First, it's a medium of exchange.

- Secondly, it is a unit of account.

- And third, it acts as a store of value.

Every element of society uses money as a means of exchange. For example, producers sell their products to wholesalers (in exchange for money). Subsequently, wholesalers sell their products to consumers.

In short, money facilitates exchanges in the economy.

It also acts as a unit of account. In other words, we use it to measure the value of various goods and services in an economy. It essentially serves as a standard of value.

Before money existed (when barter was the primary means by which people traded), it was difficult to store surplus value. Today, however, people can store surplus purchasing power and use it at any time.

What is money management?

Money management is a strategic technique employed to make money yield the highest interest value for any amount spent. In other words, it refers to how a person handles all aspects of their finances, from budgeting for the destination of each paycheck to setting long-term investment goals that will help them reach those goals. Money management is not just about saying "no" to any purchase but developing a plan that allows you to say "yes" to the things that are most important to you. Any amount of money can be too small if you don't have good money management skills.

Objectives of money management

Objectives can be:

- ✓ Ensure a regular and adequate supply of funds to the company.

- ✓ Ensure adequate returns for shareholders who will depend on the earning capacity, the market price of the share, the expectations of shareholders.

- ✓ Ensure optimal use of funds. Once funds are obtained, they should be used as much as possible at the lowest cost.

- ✓ Promote investment security, i.e. funds must be invested in secure enterprises in order to achieve an appropriate rate of return.

- ✓ Plan a sound capital structure: there must be a sound and fair composition of capital to maintain a balance between debt and equity.

Key points for good money management

- Knowing where you are

The beginning of good money management requires you to know where you are in terms of assets (things you own) and liabilities (amounts you owe). Your assets include your bank accounts, investment accounts, retirement accounts and property, such as your home and car. Your liabilities include your credit card balances, student loans, car loans, mortgages and other debts. When you subtract your assets from your liabilities, you get your net worth. If your liabilities are more than your assets, your net worth is negative. But with good money management, you can change that.

- Establishing objectives

Objectives help us define how we should manage our money. It's easy to overlook long-term goals in favor of trying to figure out what bills are being paid today. However, by setting goals, you can give clarity about which expenses are necessary and which you can cut. There is no universal "good" and "bad" in terms of your spending goals, but an effort is needed to achieve them. For example, if it is your dream to have a car that costs $25,000, you must make more spending cuts than someone who just wants to spend $10,000 on a car.

- Creating and Adjusting the Budget

Creating a budget helps you stay on top of money management because you set aside certain amounts for certain expenses. For example, it may be limited to $200 for entertainment each month after taking into account other basic needs and debt payments. However, your budget can be a moving target over time. If you realize you can buy groceries on sale and save $50 a month, you can increase your entertainment budget to $225 and add $25 to your savings budget. Alternatively, if you get a pay raise, make a budget that increases your savings rather than adding it to discretionary spending amounts.

- Manage multiple accounts

As you save for different goals, you're likely to have money in several accounts. For example, you can keep your emergency fund in a separate savings account, so you are not tempted to use it for impulse buying. You will also use different strategies for objectives with different time horizons. You may be more aggressive by investing in stocks and bonds with funds in your retirement account if you don't need the money for 30 years. On the other hand, you'll want a risk-free account, such as a savings account, for your emergency fund because you could need that money at any time. A software program, like Quicken, can help you track your various accounts to make sure you keep up with your spending and savings goals.

Money Management Techniques

1. Avoid any unnecessary expenses.

2. Always opt for the most profitable alternative.

3. Increase interest expenses more than anything else.

4. Establish the expected benefits of each desired expense by using the plus/minus/zero canon to the standard of living value system.

All these techniques are aimed at boosting investment and multiplying the portfolio.

Chapter 2: Creating a Budget

What is a budget?

Budgeting is planning how you are going to use the money you earn. It includes a list of expenses for which it is responsible. Budgeting helps you see if you still have money left after paying for all your expenses. Estimate the amount of income and expenses you may experience in a future period.

A budget represents your financial position. It's a good way to see if you're financially in a good place to live comfortably and debt free.

The word budget, however, has a slightly different meaning to "having a budget". Budgeting is when you provide or reserve a certain amount of money for a specific purpose. Therefore, you may be budgeting for a house, a car, etc., which is often referred to as savings.

The budget studies and calculates the entry of resources, the costs and the times in which these passes through the productive process, the time of sale, the time of collection of the cash and the circularity with which these return to produce new resources, to show in the end the profitability of the circularized resources made available.

Why make a budget?

Tracking our spending gives us a strong sense of where our money is going and can help us reach our financial goals.

The budget is a continuous guide that must be continually monitored and evaluated. Each year the old budget must be evaluated, and the new budget must be planned.

Advantages of making a budget

The budget plays an important role in the effective use of resources and in achieving the overall objectives of the organization.

It has the following advantages:

1. The budget forces and motivates management to make an early and timely study of their problems. It generates a sense of caution and care, and a proper study among managers before they make decisions.

2. The budget provides a valuable means to control the income and expenses of a company or of oneself, since it is a "plan of expenses".

3. The budget provides a tool through which management policies and objectives are

periodically evaluated, tested and set as guidelines for the entire organization.

4. The budget helps direct capital and other resources to the most profitable channels.

5. The budget makes it possible to decentralize responsibility without losing control of the business. It reveals weaknesses, inefficiencies, deviations in the organization very quickly that can be verified immediately to achieve the desired goal.

6. The use of the budget in an organization develops a "cost consciousness" attitude, stimulates the effective use of resources, and creates a for-profit environment throughout the organization. Emphasizes how much must be spent to achieve an objective.

7. Provides a standard, basis or criterion for measuring the performance of departments and individuals working in organizations. Individual managers can evaluate their own decisions and achievements and take appropriate action to improve their performance.

8. Budgeting fosters productive competition provides incentives to perform efficiently and gives a sense of purpose to every individual in the organization. All these positive factors lead to

increased production and increase employee productivity.

9. The budget provides a systematic and disciplined approach to problem solving in the organization.

10. The budget is executed in almost all enterprises, helping the total national economy by providing stability in employment, economic use of resources and effective waste prevention.

Limitations or disadvantages of making a budget:

While budgeting performs many functions and has many advantages that are vital to an organization, it has certain limitations that require careful consideration:

1. Planning, budgeting, or forecasting is not an exact science; it uses approximations and judgments that may not be one hundred percent accurate. At best, a budget is an estimate; no one knows precisely what will happen in the future.

2. The success of the budget depends on the cooperation and participation of all members of management. All people should direct their efforts according to the plan. Senior management must also comply with the budget and provide cooperation. Many times, budgeting

has failed because executive management has only paid attention to its execution.

3. A budget is only a tool and does not eliminate or take the place of administration. A budget cannot be replaced by administration but should only be used by administration to perform management functions. Executives generally feel "surrounded" by a budget and its related figures. They do not understand that the budget is intended to provide detailed information, goals and objectives that can help them achieve the company's objectives.

4. Establishing a budget process takes time. In addition, sometimes too much is expected of a budget and, if expectations are not met, the blame lies with the budget. An efficient budgeting program requires that those responsible understand the philosophy, objectives, and essential elements of the budget.

5. Overemphasis on budgeting can lead to attempts by lower-level management and employees to alter the system by providing inaccurate estimates of future costs and revenues, and by not taking advantage of changes in the environment because doing so would lead to a deviation from the plan, they would be considered operational contrary to the budget. Under an unbalanced budget program,

employees will tend to overestimate costs and underestimate revenues, thus creating budget looseness.

6. As the end of the budget period approaches and employees realize that actual expenditures have not been as large as those allowed by the budget, there may be a temptation to spend excessive amounts to "exhaust" the budget allocation. Such activities result in low profits for the company.

Obstacles to budgeting

- Lack of discipline.

- To think it doesn't matter.

- To be trusting, to think that family or someone else will send us more money.

Recommendations for a successful budget

- Identify all sources and amounts of revenue.

- Identify how dollars are spent today.

- Calculate budget amounts

- Set goals and make adjustments.

Steps to making a sound budget plan.

Every great financial plan starts with a solid budget. If you're trying to pay bills or save for a dream vacation, a budget is the first step to making your financial goals a reality. Follow these steps to set up a realistic budget that takes you where you want to go.

1. Calculate expenses

Your first business is to find out exactly how much you spend each month. Do this by consulting your bank statements, receipts and financial records. Because some expenses are intermittent, such as insurance payments, you'll get the most accurate financial picture by averaging six months to a year. Add up everything you spent during the past six to 12 months and then divide by the number of months, which will give you your average monthly expenses.

Remember that being thorough when adding up expenses is important to creating a realistic budget. A forgotten invoice really puts a key in your savings plan. When calculating your expenses, also consider unexpected bills, such as unplanned auto repairs. A good rule of thumb is to add an additional 10 percent to 15 percent. So, if you've determined that you spend $1,500 a month, add $150 to $225.

2. Determine Your Income

Once you've figured out how much money you need to stay afloat financially each month, it's time to determine your actual income. In addition to your regular salary, get an accurate picture by adding additional funds presented to you throughout the year, such as cash gifts, online item sales, or garage sales, and don't forget other sources of income such as alimony, child support, interest, dividends, and rental income.

3. Set savings and debt repayment goals

To determine realistic savings and debt repayment goals, you need to find out if you have a deficit or overbudget. Do this by subtracting your monthly expenses from your income. If you determine you're making more money than you're spending, congratulations. This amount can be used for savings and debt repayment.

But if you determine that you're spending more than you're earning, it's time to make some cuts so you have something to save and don't get into debt anymore. The best way to find out where you can reduce your expenses is to keep track of your expenses and record them for a month. Seemingly insignificant items, such as a cup of coffee, accumulate over time. For example, even if you spend only $5 a week on snacks, that adds up to $260 a year, which is not insignificant.

Once you have a clear idea of where all your money is going, be relentless in reducing expenses until your budget is stabilized. Cut back enough so you have 10 to 20 percent of your income left each month to add to your savings account. If you can't cut back enough on your budget, consider ways to increase your income.

4. Expense recording and progress tracking

The best way to stay above your budget is to record all your expenses and income. Having to enter expenses will make you think twice before you waste, and it is especially satisfying and motivating to record when you have reached a savings goal.

5. Be realistic

Try to stick to your budget most of the time and you will surely reach your financial goals. Breaking your budget occasionally is fine, as long as you get back to normal as soon as possible.

Chapter 3: Establishing Savings

What is savings?

Saving is not the absence of expense. It is defined as the intentional act of setting money aside for a specific purpose or objective. Trust also states that savings is the percentage of income that is not spent and is set aside for future needs through various financial mechanisms.

What does it mean to save money?

Saving money is saving money for something. For example, save money to buy a car or a house or even a pair of shoes. It is the process of taking part of your income and reserving for future use.

The extent to which you save depends on your preferences for future consumption over the present. Saving would be similar to budgeting for something specific. In one sentence, they would mean the same thing.

Savings and Budgets

The budget comes into play for many people who want to save a certain amount of money, such as a down payment on a house, money for a new car, or gifts for vacations.

One system that works in practice is to set aside the amount you want to save at the beginning of the month, because in this way we will face the weakness of our human nature, which will try to betray the goal proposed, transferring to consumption the surplus intended for saving. One is mentally programmed to pay the debts first, at the moment of receiving the end of the month salary, since the "system" will not give him truce, ordering him to keep the payments of the acquired commitments up to date, or otherwise, he will be expelled from it. This fear causes that when we receive the salary, one ends up paying them all, except oneself, who is the one who worked to earn that money. Remember that it's legitimate for a portion of what you earn to be for you to save, says Trust.

Once you've defined what you're saving for, how much you need to save, and when you need that money, you can create a budget or roadmap that will help you save the right amount for your important financial goals.

Some examples of savings goals include:

- Build an emergency fund.

- Save for Christmas celebrations or special gifts.

- Save 10% to 15% of your income for retirement.

- Reserving $40 per month for future auto repairs.

- Create a college fund for your children (or yourself).

- Have enough money available to cover all of your insurance deductibles (health insurance, homeowners or renter's insurance, disability insurance) so that if you need to make a claim, you can easily pay the deductible without worry.

Budget vs. Money Saving

There's almost no difference between the two. "I'm budgeting for a car" vs. "I'm saving for a car" is the same thing. However, "saving" is not the same as "budgeting. Budgeting helps you save.

Saving is saving money. A budget is a spending plan.

Why is saving important?

It is important to save money for the following reasons:

Become financially independent

It means having the freedom to make decisions in your life other than winning a paycheck.

To get out of debt

If you ever want to get out of debt, you must save some money. Sounds ironic, doesn't it? However, credit cards will never be paid for if you must continue to use them for every "emergency" that arises.

Cover annual expenses

If you want to have a good, relatively stress-free financial life, you should save for annual expenses. These may include money for gifts, vacations, vehicle maintenance, minor home repairs, appliance repairs, property taxes, and possibly income taxes.

Unforeseen expenses

You can't always count on the bank to lend you money for any type of unforeseen event (an accident, losing your job, repairing the car, etc.) It's much better to anticipate the worst case and save some money.

Have a good life

There are great emotional, psychological and physical consequences to living always stressed. Therefore, being organized won't make you happy on your own, but it can surely help. There is so much in your future that you have no control over, so setting aside some money to spend when you need it is to organize and take control of your future and your financial affairs.

Disadvantages of saving money

Let's start with the disadvantages.

First, saving money means you're not spending it. And it's possible to be too frugal. Are you doing things like skipping dental appointments not because you can't afford them but because you want to save money? That's too frugal. Sure, save now, but if you end up needing a root canal, it will cost you a lot more. Preventive care is worth it.

If you focus too much on saving money, you could make bad decisions when it comes to spending. You can save money by hiring the cheapest contractor to build your fence, and then get caught with a fence that falls the following year during a storm. Sure, he saved money up front, but was it worth it?

You can also miss experiences because you're saving money. All your friends go to a concert you want to go to, but you decide you need to save money. That could be a definite nuisance. And if you're always saving, probably never travel, and I think everyone should take the opportunity to travel, either within their own country or internationally. Take the time to take a break. Being stuck saving the home is one of the disadvantages of saving money.

You definitely don't want to discover in your 90's that you never leave home, that you don't seem to have any money, that you never travel, that you never buy anything nice and live like a poor man, but when you die, it turns out that you have millions in the bank. You have to have some kind of balance.

Overall, I think everyone should have a little fun money in their budget. Even if you're trying to achieve a savings goal, you need to have a little money you can spend on something you want, whether it's movie tickets or downloadable music or a night out in the city.

Advantages of saving money

Of course, for every disadvantage of saving money, there is an advantage.

The great advantage of saving money is that you are prepared when you need to spend it. Let's say that after your cheap fence falls, you decide to spend the money to repair it properly. Definitive victory.

By saving money, even small amounts at a time, it's possible that someday you could make a big purchase without having to finance it. Wouldn't it be nice to be able to buy a car in cash and not have to pay a loan? Wouldn't it be amazing to be able to buy a house in cash and not have to pay a mortgage? (Well, then this is less likely, but depending on where you live, it's certainly possible).

If you are saving your money in a bank account or on CD, you will also earn money by saving it. All that interest adds up. And you can invest some of that money and help it keep growing.

For me, the key is to balance the advantages and disadvantages of saving money. Save, but not too much.

Don't let that early retirement dream mean you're living in a dilapidated cabin. Find the balance between your savings goals and your spending needs and wants.

Chapter 4: Debts

What is a debt?

It is a compulsory payment commitment between two entities (they can be individuals, groups, companies, the State).

The Debt Collection Process

The debt collection process begins when you miss a payment on a credit card or loan. The debtor has 30 days from the invoice due date (not the invoice date) to make payment before informing the credit bureaus. During this time, the creditor will attempt to contact the debtor by telephone, e-mail, or letter to receive payment and any late charges. It is best to take care of the debt during this 30-day period. The debtor can explain his situation and establish a payment plan.

After 30 days, the debt is transferred to another department of the same company that specializes in recovering the delinquent debt. This is not a collection agency, just a department within the loan company. They could report your delinquency to a credit bureau and close your credit card account.

After 180 days, the creditor will generally take the debt or cancel it from his books and sell it to a debt collection agency. Keep in mind that the creditor could contract or sell the debt at any time before the 180 days, so it is best to act as soon as possible.

Tips for Getting Out of Debt

Before you start "attacking" your debts, the first step is to save a good amount of money to have an emergency fund. What is an emergency fund? When unexpected events and situations arise such as accidents, travel, car repairs or anything else that involves a large expense, the most common is that we end up in debt because at the moment we do not have enough money to cover those expenses.

On the other hand, if we have an emergency fund, we would not accumulate more debt if we had to make an unexpected expense.

1. Start your own business.

Starting your own business has never been easier! Do you have a gift for doing things? Sell your products online! Are you an animal lover? Take a dog walk or take care of pets. Do you have a good eye and a good camera? Start accepting clients for photo shoots.

2. Get a part-time job.

Don't you want to start your own business? Then consider becoming a driver for Lyft or Uber. A pizza delivery job at night could also bring extra money. You can even deliver other types of food in your spare time by working for places like UberEATS or Grubhub app. Of course, you'll have to give up your pride and give up some nights and weekends of inactivity. But that's a small sacrifice for extra money in his pocket.

3. Sell the car!

The average monthly payment on a new car is $523. That's just outrageous! How much faster could your snowball move debt if you applied that $500 each month?

4. Cut your credit cards.

Destroy them, burn them, shoot them. You will never get out of debt until you stop making debt a way of life.

5. Use the envelope system.

When you pay cash, *you* really *feel like* your money is getting out of hand. Ow! Nobody likes that. People tend to spend less when they pay cold, hard cash. With the envelope system, you'll see that cash is shrinking so you can keep track of how much you're spending.

6. Stop investing.

Yeah, you read that right. And yes, we even mean to stop contributing to your 401(k). At this point, you want all of your income to go out of debt. Once you are debt free and have saved three to six months of expenses in an emergency fund, you can resume your contributions. By then, you can start spending 15% of your income on retirement.

7.   Ignore your broken friends.

Stop trying to keep up with the Joneses! Remember that you are now living like no one else and then you can live like no one else! In 20 years, you won't have a financial worry in the world, while everyone else will have loans for cars, mortgages and credit card bills.

8.   Make a budget!

The budget must be easy and, we dare say it, fun! Focus your money on what matters: daily expenses, those annoying debts, and wealth creation.

9.   Tell the kids you have a limited budget.

When it comes to money, kids can be a worse guide than their stomach. Be open with them about what *you're doing* and you *don't* have space in the budget. And remember, never be afraid to use that magic word, "no."

Advantages versus disadvantages of debt financing

Advantages

- **Retain control.**   When you accept debt financing from a lending institution, the lender has no say in how you run your business. You make all the decisions. The business relationship ends once you have paid the loan in full.

- **Tax advantage.** The amount you pay in interest is tax deductible, effectively reducing your net obligation.

- **Easier planning.** You know in advance exactly how much principal and interest you will pay each month. This makes it easier to budget and make financial plans.

Disadvantages

Debt financing has its limitations and disadvantages.

Qualification requirements. You need a good enough credit rating to receive financing.

- **Discipline.** You must have the financial discipline to make payments on time. Exercise moderation and use good financial judgment when using debt. A business that depends too much on debt could be seen as 'high risk' by potential investors, and that could limit access to capital financing at some point.

- **Collateral.** By agreeing to provide collateral to the lender, you could jeopardize some business assets. You may also be required to personally guarantee the loan, putting your own assets at risk.

Decisive factor

- How important is it for you to maintain total control of the business?

- How important is it to know exactly what you will owe in monthly payments?

- Are you comfortable making regular monthly payments?

- Are you able to qualify for debt financing? What is your credit history like? Does it have a good credit rating?

- Do you have any warranties I can use? Do you feel comfortable using it?

Chapter 5: Investing

What is investing?

It is defined as the placement of financial resources that the company makes to obtain a return from them or receive dividends that help to increase the capital of the company.

Why is it important?

When you invest, you are committing money or another resource to the expectation of some future benefit. A college education, for example, may be considered an investment because you invest your time (a resource) in hopes of getting a degree and a good job after graduation (the future benefit). In a financial sense, investing means that an individual commits money to a financial asset, or security, such as a stock or bond, in the hope of receiving even more money in the future. The potential to receive more money later is the reason people invest first.

How do investments make money?

Most investments earn money for an investor through appreciation, interest payments or dividends. Appreciation means that the value of an asset has increased. If you bought a collectible for $100 and five years later it was worth $500, then the collectible value was appreciated. Securities can do the same: a share issued by a company can increase in value over several years.

You probably paid the interest on a loan you got, whether it was a student loan or a mortgage. These interest payments you paid to the lender were how the lender earned money on that loan (or investment). A type of security that issues interest payments to its investors is a bond. When you buy a bond, you are lending money to the government or a corporation, which promises to reimburse you and make interest payments on the amount you lent.

Dividends are also issued as a payment to investors but are made by companies whose shares or equity are owned by them. Public companies issue shares to raise money for commercial activities, allowing investors to buy these shares. If you own a share in a company, that company may also issue dividend payments to you as a way to share your profits with your investors. This is in addition to any appreciation in the value of the shares.

Investment risks

Although investing can make increase your wealth, it comes with a risk. The biggest risk with investing is that you may lose the money you invested. Unlike checking or savings accounts, the value of which is guaranteed by the Federal Deposit Insurance Corporation (FDIC), investments do not have that guarantee.

Some investments are less risky than others, but all investments carry some risk. The amount of risk also affects the rate of return on an investment, which means that someone assumes many risks, there must also be the possibility of a great reward. Think about it: you wouldn't take a big risk without the possibility of a big reward. Conversely, investments with less risk tend to have lower returns.

One-way investors reduce their overall risk is by investing in a variety of different securities, such as stocks and bonds, or even different types of the same security, such as government bonds and corporate bonds. This is known as diversification and is an important concept that any investor should understand.

Another big risk when investing is your own emotions. Many investments are volatile in the short term, which means that their value can fluctuate greatly between one and five years. During economic downturns, the value of many investments can fall dramatically. As an investor, it's hard to see your investments lose money. This can lead to investment decisions based on fear or panic, such as selling stocks when prices fall too low for your convenience.

When you invest, you must keep most of your investments for ten, twenty, or more years. It is during these longer periods of time that the value of investments has historically increased. Keep this in mind when making investment decisions. You will perform better as an investor if your investment decisions are based on logic and reason rather than emotion.

You may have heard of investing compared to gambling, and if you invest in an unfavorable way, it may be the same. However, smart investors will approach investing strategically to choose investments that have a good expectation of return. The game, on the other hand, is usually based purely on chance.

Why does it matter to invest?

When you think of investing in terms of capitalization and time, it's easy to understand why people would risk their money for a possible return. You may remember learning about compound interest in math class, but the principle is simple: the yields you earn with money can be compound, and then they begin to earn yields as well. When you give your money enough time to capitalize, growth can become exponential.

How to start investing?

The advent of online investing has made it easier to start investing. Many online brokers don't require a minimum amount to start, so you can start with as little as $50. Some types of brokers, such as full-service brokers, will select your investments for a truly straightforward approach. Keep in mind that all brokers charge a variety of fees to use their services; you must understand them before you register.

You should also understand what type of account you will open, how much you have to invest, and what you will invest in. Most new investors say it would be prudent to invest in low-cost index mutual funds and ETFs instead of choosing specific stocks or bonds. This is because the funds allow you to have a portion of tens or hundreds of different stocks and many are well diversified and affordable. With whatever strategy you choose, be sure to investigate and understand all the risks involved.

Chapter 6: Money Theories

The system of T. Harv Eker's money jars

T. Harv Eker sums it up with these wise words: "The habit of managing your money is more important than the amount. And this is one of 17 factors that differentiates rich people from poor people.

Many people try to enrich themselves by emulating Warren Buffett's multimillion-dollar investment strategy. It's great, although they miss (or choose to ignore) an important ingredient, one of the reasons Buffett is so rich is because it's also infamously frugal.

There are numerous examples of Buffett's frugality. For example, when her first child was born, Buffett turned a drawer into a bassinet. For her second child, she borrowed a crib. He drove a Volkswagen until his wife upgraded it to a Cadillac (which she felt was better for her image). Buffett still lives in Omaha, Nebraska, in the house he bought for $31,500 more than 50 years ago. You understand the drift ...

Buffett manages his money and wealth with the principle that small sums are made up. Every penny not spent today means a lot more money to invest or use in the future. In the book The Millionaire Next Door , Stanley and Danko also found some interesting truths about the many millionaire homes they described in the United

States: most of the millionaire homes they described did not have extravagant lifestyles and luxury items like brand name watches, suits, automobiles, etc.). They accumulate so much wealth precisely because they live *below* their means.

T. Harv Eker sums it up with these wise words: "The habit of managing your money is more important than the amount. And this is one of 17 factors that differentiates rich people from poor people.

The concept of 6 jars for wealth management

The idea of this system is simple: separate your income into 6 different accounts for specific purposes. You can also use physical bottles, envelopes, etc. and label them accordingly. The most important thing is to constantly deposit into these jars/accounts as follows:

❖ Needs (50%):

Half of your income goes to real needs (N) such as food, mortgage payments, bills, gas, oil, insurance, etc. If you can't meet all of your needs with 50% of your income, you should do one (or both) of these things:

- Simplify your life: find out how you can spend less

- Earn more: find out how you can earn more

❖ Financial freedom account (10%):

10% of your income goes to your Financial Freedom (LF) bottle. The money in this jar can *only be* used for investments (with yields or profits). This bottle is used to generate wealth for your future financial freedom. You must *not* spend this money.

❖ Long-term savings (10%):

10% of your income goes to the Long-Term Savings (LTP) bottle for expenses. The aim of this bottle is to save money for future expenses (e.g. a new car, a holiday, a new sofa, gifts, paying debts, etc.)

❖ Education (10%):

Successful people invest and grow constantly. Therefore, 10% of their income goes to the bottle of Education (E). The more knowledge and skills they acquire, the greater their earning capacity. And the more you earn, the more you need to learn (how to manage your additional wealth?). How do you take your income to the next level? etc.). Use the money in this jar for personal or professional development (e.g., books, courses, seminars).

❖ Play (10%):

10% of your income goes to the game jar (J). It is important to indulge yourself once in a while with a good massage, new clothes, an elegant dinner ... To avoid overspending or underspending, be sure to use the money in this jar at least every few months. This allows you to spend without guilt and also gradually improve your standard of living as your income increases.

❖ Give (10%):

10% of your income goes to the give bottle (D). No matter how poor your circumstances, there will always be someone who is in an even more serious state. In addition to feeling good about helping others, giving away part of your income also helps you unconsciously develop a wealth mentality that has more than enough to give away.

The idea of this system is simple: first separate your income into 6 different accounts for specific purposes. You can use bank accounts or real jars, or you can also use physical jars, envelopes, etc. and label them accordingly. The most important thing is to constantly deposit into these jars or accounts as follows:

Starting to apply the 6 pitchers

Here are 3 simple steps to get started:

First, know your percentages. You can't manage your money without knowing how much you earn and spend. You can start by calculating your current monthly income and the amount that will be placed in each of the 6 vials. Then record how much money you spend each day. Just knowing your spending patterns is a first step in the right direction.

Second, change your mind. Understand that money management is not about restricting your freedom; it is about eventually creating financial freedom. Several years from now, you can retire happily while your friends (who now enjoy the "good life") still struggle to pay for your expensive lifestyle. He constantly remembers out loud "I'm an excellent money manager!".

Third, don't entertain any excuses. It's easy to say, "I'll do it tomorrow" or "I don't have time for that." The big question to ask is: when do you want to be rich and financially free? If you are serious about your financial goals, then no excuses should be allowed. Start now and stick to your plan.

Warren Buffett's Theory

Warren Buffett has built his own personal fortune at more than $72 billion, making him the third richest person in the world. Not only that, it has offered a lot of common-sense advice on wealth creation that absolutely anyone can follow, whether they know something about investments or not.

❖ Never lose money.

"Rule number one: never lose money. Rule number 2: never forget rule number 1," Buffett said. Of course, this is obvious: I don't know anyone who thinks losing money is a *good* idea.

But go beyond that obviousness, and this is practical advice that is very wise: avoid risk whenever you can. In particular, he says, to be happy and successful, never risk something you need to get something you want, even if the odds are a thousand to one in your favor.

With this rule in mind, Buffett himself refrained from making many risky investments over the years and let go of what could have been big profits, for example, in technology. Over time, however, this risk aversion strategy has yielded excellent results.

❖ Get high value at a low price.

"Price is what you pay, value is what you get," Buffett wrote to Berkshire Hathaway shareholders. Therefore, you may lose money (and violate Rule No. 1) if you end up paying more for something worth its value. This can happen, for example, when you use a credit card and end up adding a lot of interest to the price of what you've bought. Or when you buy something, from a share to a real estate, when everyone else buys and the market is overpriced.

"Whether we're talking socks or stocks, I like to buy quality merchandise when it's on sale," Buffett wrote. It's a wise approach.

❖ Acquire healthy financial habits.

"Most behavior is habitual," Buffett said in a speech to college students, "and they say the chains of habit are too light to feel until they are too heavy to break.

We all have habits we'd like to break, and others we'd like to form. Among the latter, Buffett says, the most important thing is to save money. "The biggest mistake is not learning the habit of saving properly," he says. Consider using automatic deductions from your paycheck or automatic transfers from your checking account to a savings or investment account to make this good habit as simple as possible.

❖ Have plenty of cash available.

Buffett says Berkshire Hathaway always has at least $20 billion, and generally much more, in cash equivalents, ready to be used in case of need. Once again, this is a very risk-averse strategy that means sacrificing the higher profits you could have made by investing that money. But it kept the company out of trouble during the 2008 financial recession when so many others had problems or failed.

Don't you have $20 billion to hide in your mattress? It is still a very good idea to have a decent portion of your money in cash or money market accounts, or items such as U.S. Treasury bills. This is especially important if you are an entrepreneur and may have an uncertain income. As Buffett says, cash is for a business-like oxygen for a body: "I never thought of it when it was present, the only thing in mind when it is absent.

❖ Invest in yourself.

Buffett has often said that you must invest in yourself as much as you can, and in every way you can, from taking care of your body to finding the job you love to education. "Everything you do to improve your own talents and make yourself more valuable will be rewarded in terms of appropriate real purchasing power," he said in an interview. Those returns will be multiplied by 10, and unlike other assets, you cannot have your skills and abilities taken away.

That could mean going to school, or it could mean taking a training position, starting your own business, or even taking a volunteer position if you taught him some skills he didn't have before. What makes you smarter makes you richer.

❖ Set long-term goals.

The mistake most people make is that they try to catch any wave of rising prices and the quick returns they think they see in the short term, says Buffett. That kind of thinking almost always puts people in trouble. On the other hand, he advises, "to invest with a horizon of several decades". Instead of trying to make quick money, you should focus on increasing your purchasing power throughout your life. That sounds like a very sensible approach to me.

Action steps: inspired by Warren Buffett

- o Save money by deciding where to skimp and where to waste.

- o Start diverting part of your income to an investment account.

- o Record income and expenses and create a spending plan.

Chapter 7: Financial Freedom

What is financial freedom?

Freedom is an abstract term. It's hard to define, but one thing is for sure: everyone knows they love it. No one wants to have to depend on someone else to manage their finances or provide them with money when they need it. Everyone wants to stand up and make a living without the help of friends or family.

Financial freedom is the freedom to stop having financial stress. It is the ability to make monetary stress fly away as if it never existed.

What does it mean to be financially independent?

It means you can take a day off from work when you're sick without worrying about being chased by a creditor at the end of the month. It also means you don't have to filter phone calls to avoid bad news regarding finances.

Benefits of financial freedom

There are a lot of benefits you get when you reach a certain level of financial freedom. Taking long-term benefits into account will help you stay on track as you work toward your financial goals.

These are some of the main benefits of financial independence:

- ✓ **Freedom from debt**: Imagine a life without debt. With no credit card loans to pay off, no outstanding mortgages, all your income goes toward growing your cash reserve and investments. I hear you say that world doesn't exist. It does exist. To get there, you just have to learn to spend less than you earn.

- ✓ **Freedom to do whatever you want**: When you are not at the mercy of creditors, you can do a lot. For example, you can start your own business, move to another city or country, or make other important decisions. The extra money and lack of credit card bills will allow you to start new hobbies. Maybe that's as simple as using some extra money to learn to play a musical instrument.

- ✓ **Time**: When in debt, many people have to do extra work to pay their bills. In this situation, time becomes a precious commodity that cannot be used simply as a person sees fit. With the extra time allowed by the lack of financial problems, a myriad of things can be done.

- ✓ **Freedom from financial stress**: when it comes to getting out of debt, a person becomes patient out of necessity. There is nothing worse than someone who is indebted and impatient, because they will always make the wrong decisions when it comes to buying items. Patients will allow you to delay consumption now to maintain peace of mind.

✓ **Freedom to increase your savings:** Why save when you'll only get a little interest on your savings? Here's my answer. Saving is a natural thing that happens when you spend less than you have. In other words, if your income exceeds your expenses, you'll have cash that you can then do as you please. You save to build a healthy cash reserve and you save to have the money to take advantage of the investment opportunities presented to you. For example, having the necessary deposit for a mortgage.

✓ **Freedom to start creating wealth:** In short, creating wealth is what will give you financial freedom. But you can only create wealth if you have a positive cash flow that allows you to take the steps. Creating wealth involves risks, so you should seek the advice of qualified professionals before deciding to invest your hard-earned money in an investment.

✓ *Unemployment Insurance:* Having savings and investments in place means you don't need to rely on minimum unemployment payments that only cover basic needs; you can continue to live a lifestyle that is comfortable for you.

- ✓ **Extra spending power:** Your assets and investments can generate additional income you wouldn't otherwise receive; consider it a bonus, in addition to your salary, that you can pay yourself.

- ✓ **Early retirement:** Early retirement is an attractive option if you can afford it. If good investment decisions mean you can live on dividends, early retirement could become a reality, not just a dream.

- ✓ **Peace of mind:** If your passive income exceeds your minimum expenses, you will have greater flexibility. How much less stress will you experience? And with less stress comes the peace and freedom to live life on your own terms.

Why is it so hard to achieve financial freedom?

Most people want to be financially independent, so why do so few people get there?

One of the secrets to financial independence is to accept that it usually "just doesn't happen. It starts with a detailed plan and the willingness to commit to that plan.

A good starting point is to review your current assets and investments. Are they giving you the best possible returns? Review what liabilities or debts you have, what changes could you make to reduce them now? These are some of the cornerstones of a sound financial plan.

Regardless of where you are in life, whether you're just getting started, enjoying maximum earning potential, or thinking about taking life a little easier, financial planning isn't just important, it's essential.

Keep in mind that healthier lifestyles and medical advancements can add ten or more years to our life expectancy, which we may not have considered when we started working. Another good reason to consider becoming financially independent sooner rather than later.

Tips for Achieving Financial Freedom

If you haven't already done so, now would be a good time to consider embarking on the path that leads to financial freedom. Pay off the highest interest debt you owe. Try and consolidate all your debts in one place if possible. Start an emergency fund. Look for ways to take on more responsibility at work or look for a job that has a higher pay rate. While it's easy to feel overwhelmed by all the things listed in this short article, the key is to commit to your goals every day and realize that you can't do everything all at once. Anything you do to improve your current financial situation can improve your life and make sure you're prepared for future financial difficulties.

It is important to remember that money problems are not the end of the world. Applying a little common sense to financial problems is often all that is needed to get back on track and avoid the problems associated with poor finances. Now nothing prevents you from achieving financial independence: this site is a free resource to help you get started!

Bibliographic References

Trust S. (2006). Money and savings. Retrieved from https://www.pinturayartistas.com/wordpress/wp-content/uploads/libros/El%20c%F3digo%20del%20dinero.pdf

Rincon, C. (2011). Business budgets. Recovered from

https://www.academia.edu/35646497/Presupuestos-empresariales

Rodriguez, A. (2008). Step by Step How to get out of debt successfully in no time. Retrieved from https://s3.amazonaws.com/deudasbusta19/LibroDeudasNuncaMasBusta1.pdf

Bodoo, S. (2014). The road to financial freedom. Retrieved from https://books.google.com.pe/books?id=Sz2lAwAAQBAJrintsec=frontcoverq=libertad+financiera&hl=en&sa=X&ved=0ahUKEwiYsrmFs4vlAhUEvFkKHb-KDAAQ6AEIKzAA#v=onepage&q=libertad%20financiera&f=false

Bernstein, W. (2013). Investments and investors. Retrieved from http://www.economia.unam.mx/profesores/blopez/Riesgo-Pres3.pdf

Sánchez, M. (2013). The Phoenix carpenter. Retrieved from

https://books.google.com.pe/books?id=VbUX
AwAQBAJ&pg=PT142&dq=%EF%83%98%0
9The+system+of+the+delays+of+money+T+
Harv+Eker+Books&hl=en&sa=X&&.ved=0ah
UKEwiU34fdp6TlAhVEpFkHbvWBboQ6AEI
KDAA#v=onepage&q=%EF%83%98%09%2
0system%20of%20the%20tards%20of%20mon
ey%20of%20T%20Harv%20Eker%20Books&f
=false